SONIA SERVIDA

The Story of
RENAISSANCE ARCHITECTURE

PRESTEL
Munich · London · New York

CONTENTS

INTRODUCTION

The term 'Renaissance' is used to denote the transformation in the arts that began in Italy in the early 15th century. The term was coined in the 19th century and began to enjoy greater currency with the publication of Swiss historian, Jacob Burckhardt's, famous work, *The Civilization of the Renaissance in Italy*, which dealt at great length with the concept of rebirth and the break with the mores and values of the Middle Ages. The great artistic and cultural renewal that typified the 15th and 16th centuries should, however, be considered within the context of the changes that were paving the way for the Modern Era. The European economic recovery following the 14th century political crisis saw the consolidation of a new secular class that grew wealthy through trade and transformed their cities with new public and private works.

Politically speaking, there were two different dimensions: the great monarchies, France, Spain and England, which tended to unify their territories, centralising political power to an even greater extent, to the detriment of the great feudal lords; and Italy which, on the contrary, was witnessing the extreme fragmentation of its jurisdictions and was seeing the political power once harnessed by local municipalities gradually being taken over by a system of principalities. This, however, could not forestall the unifying evolution of intellectual thinking, which found fertile ground for dissemination in Italian cities and courts which felt united by their grand Roman past — the ideal ethic of virtue and democracy.

The study of classical literature was resumed, inspired by the secular scholars working for town municipalities and princedoms. There was a rediscovery of ancient authors, their works were analysed from a philological angle and were responsible for spreading the concept of Roman Italianism, a myth that first surfaced and flourished during the 14th century, but which, largely through humanist propaganda, also became accessible beyond élite circles. The awareness of this artistic renewal, which had first begun to burgeon with the artists, Giotto di Bondone and Giovanni Boccaccio, in the 14th century, became openly conceptualised during the following century. Filippo Brunelleschi, Leon Battista Alberti, Donato Bramante and later Andrea Palladio were fully conscious of the fact that they were launching a completely different, distinct style, breaking with the recent past and reinventing the ancient classical shapes.

Religious architecture

As in so many of the great historic eras of the past, religious buildings were considered to be the most important and most representative of all, because of their symbolic meaning and their distinctive associations with the community they served. The primary role of religious buildings, besides the quantity and quality of the work, was made evident in many theoretical writings from Alberti's *De Re Aedificatoria* onwards. Alberti's publication included a detailed plan for building the ideal church, which Florentine architects saw as the most important building in any city, whose beauty was capable of drawing the populace closer to God.

Leonardo da Vinci, Canon of Proportions (Vitruvian Man), Venice, Gallerie dell'Accademia

The figure of a man, inscribed in a circle, which recurs in Renaissance drawings, is a representation of the humanist and vitruvian principle, which states that human proportions are the source of the perfect measurement of all natural things.

The rediscovery of the classical style during the early 15th century also inspired church architects to refer back to Vitruvius's treaty and to create churches along the lines of the pagan temples so extensively described in *De Architectura*. The Renaissance architects also retained many medieval buildings from the Roman era, such as the Baptistery in Florence, long believed to be the Pagan Temple of Mars and the church of Santo Stefano Rotondo in Rome, believed to be the Temple of Faunus. Brunelleschi's contemporaries found no shortage of ancient and Late Antique buildings to study, but they were also inspired by buildings from the recent past, such as the Basilica of Santa Maria del Fiore, in which the broad, centralised plan of the tribune area had a significant influence on future designs for basilicas, demonstrating that some of the concepts central to Renaissance works had previously been employed in 14th century buildings. The earliest churches to be built in the updated Renaissance style were works by the lucid, revolutionary hand of the sculptor/architect, Brunelleschi, who rationalised medieval space through the *all'antica* vocabulary. In the churches of San Lorenzo and, especially, Santo Spirito in Florence, Brunelleschi drew on the longitudinal typology typical of Italian monastic architecture, achieving a plan that was to become the prototype for religious buildings over the next few centuries. The nave of Santo

opposite page
Filippo Brunelleschi, San Lorenzo, 1540s, Florence

The church of San Lorenzo, rebuilt as part of the Medici renovation of the complex, was the first Renaissance work to have been carried out according to the principles of spatial regularisation and modularity. Working from traditional medieval plans for Italian convent basilicas, Brunelleschi's design was for a building with three aisles, a protruding transept surrounded by chapels and a cupola over the crossing where the arms of the building converged. The internal layout was determined by the use of the classical system of engaged orders applied to the arches, derived from the morphology of Roman monuments. This was to become the basis for architectural plans throughout the Renaissance era.

Constantine's Arch, 312–314 A.D., Rome

The architectural system that involves intersecting the motif of the arch with taller orders at either side, typical of the triumphal arches in Ancient Rome, is one of the most representative and commonly used devices in Renaissance architecture, taking a variety of different forms.

Spirito was designed as a harmonious succession of regular spaces based on a modular grid, culminating in a central space surmounted by a cupola, with three identical protruding arms accommodating the transept and the choir to the rear. The form of the end of the church, or tribune, with its central plan, symmetrical along one axis, is typical of most Renaissance religious buildings and spawned what is known as the 'composite church', in which the longitudinal plan of the basilica merges with the central plan typical of a great many Roman and Late Antique churches. The Sienese architect, Francesco di Giorgio Martini, formalised the concept of the composite plan in the churches of San Bernardino in Urbino and Santa Maria delle Grazie al Calcinaio, near Cortona, as well as, theoretically, in his writings and drawings. Martini sought to demonstrate how a mixed plan relates to the human figure inscribed to scale within it according to the anthropomorphical theories Alberti had so

Francesco di Giorgio Martini, Small Circular Temples, Turin, Biblioteca Reale, antique appendix to the Codex Saluzziano, vol. 84

Antique temples with rectangular plans were very rare during the Renaissance period; it was not until Palladio that a precise study of antiquities was carried out, which focused on identifying the sacred buildings of classical Rome.
During the quattrocento, the majority of places of worship believed to have been built by the ancient masters, had a central plan. These buildings had a great influence on the vision and aspirations of the Renaissance architects. Two small circular peripteral temples stand out among the mass of ancient central-plan buildings. These temples consisted of a *cella* surrounded on the exterior by columns: one of them is situated on the Roman Forum and the other in Tivoli; both are thought to have been dedicated to the Roman god, Vesta. These widely studied prototypes were frequently remodelled in 15th century drawings and paintings and formed the basis for Bramante's Tempietto di San Pietro in Montorio.

deeply espoused. This concept was also reworked by Alberti in the church of Sant'Andrea in Mantua.

Brunelleschi's work was the first clear evidence of the architects of the Renaissance's compositional preference for circular, square and octagonal shapes. This preference was epitomised in Brunelleschi's Santa Maria degli Angeli, the design of which was also informed by his careful consultation of Vitruvius's treaty and the study of ancient Roman buildings, or buildings that were considered to be Roman, i.e. built to central plans. The Baptistery of Santa Maria del Fiore, the octagonal Roman and Late Antique mausoleums, the Pantheon and ruins from the Imperial era were all highly prized prototypes for these centrally-planned designs. Both Vitruvius and Alberti believed that the circle represented the ultimate image of the perfection of Nature, the ideal proportional module on which religious buildings should be based; a form symbolic and exalted above all others. The idea of the temple, circular and surrounded by columns is illustrated in Francesco di Giorgio's imaginary drawings of that period and the anonymous veduta of an ideal city in Urbino, which depicts an enormous circular building rising up in the middle of the composition. This is perfectly rendered in Bramante's circular Tempietto at San Pietro in Montorio, the original plan of which reflected the superimposition of the Vitruvian configuration of the circle inscribed within the square. The birth of architectural composition through drawings of plans and elevations found fertile ground for experimentation in the central-plan buildings, culminating in the large variety of symmetrical shapes achieved by juxtaposing several similar volumes. Projects of the time were often disseminated due to the series of planforms that were developed. Buildings consisting of a cen-

opposite page
Giuliano da Sangallo, Santa Maria delle Carceri, 1485, Prato

Lorenzo il Magnifico had commissioned a Greek cross layout for the church, which is an outstanding example of an ideal Renaissance religious building. The simple harmonious ratios that determine the measurements of the plan and elevation are emphasised by the elegant, linear graphic quality of the decoration, with pilasters and fasciae in pietra serena that project from the pale plasterwork and accentuate the internal structural joints. The semicircular cupola, which represents the sky, rises from a cylindrical drum that appears to be suspended above the arches in a majestic volumetric composition.

Giuliano da Sangallo, Plan for the new St Peter's Basilica, c. 1505, Florence, Gabinetto Disegni and Stampe degli Uffizi, 8A

Prior to the rise of Bramante, Giuliano da Sangallo was the favourite architect of Pope Julius II. De Sangallo took part in drawing up a new scheme for the basilica of St Peter's. His plan is now conserved in the Uffizi Gallery. The complex internal structure, based on a quincunx pattern, was concealed behind massive external walls that enclose the building in the manner of a fortified palace and are reminiscent of the huge compounds containing the Roman thermal baths, studied at length by Sangallo and reproduced by him on numerous occasions.

tral space enclosed by a cupola and symmetrically surrounded by subsidiary spaces were the focus for architectural debate in Sforza Milan, where Bramante and da Vinci were both working in a climate of high intellectual tension. The beautiful Late Antique octagonal church of San Lorenzo in Milan, surrounded by smaller satellite spaces would undoubtedly have served as an exceptional model, inspiring both architects to draw up multi-axial plans, culminating in the drawings of complex structures that can be seen in da Vinci's notebooks. Although there is a slight hint of this multi-axiality in the octagonal sacristy of Santa Maria next to San Satiro, Bramante was not to draw fully on his research until after 1500, when he created a monumental design for the Basilica of St Peter's in Rome, which he visualised as a huge structure with a central plan, incorporating the forms of the square and the cross. This led to the definition of the quincunx church, a plan articulated by five domed spaces inscribed in a Greek cross.

Giovanni Battagio, Santa Maria della Croce, 1490, Crema

The architect Giovanni Battagio, based in Lodi, was part of the circle of architects who worked on the building of San Satiro in Milan alongside Donato Bramante. Battagio utilised the concepts that were central to architectural debate during his years in Milan; a debate that was strongly influenced by the Late Antique Lombardy architects as well as da Vinci and Bramante's ideas. Bramante's church, Santa Maria della Croce epitomises these ideas: the layout for the church is a complex one, involving a central cylindrical focal structure onto which four smaller Greek cross-plan stuctures were attached.

The device of the massive transversal pier, organically inserted into the extended octagonal structure at the centre of the cross is evidence of the great spatial change that took place during the 15th century: from Brunelleschi's serene, linear compositions to Alberti's monumental Roman structure in the nave of Sant'Andrea and culminating in Bramante's plastic, strongly articulated designs.

The image of St Peter's as a sepulchral mausoleum for the chief Apostles is the absolute pinnacle of the formal and intellectual search for the ideal shape for religious buildings and was a highly significant prototype that was to enjoy widespread acknowledgement. The dissemination of Bramante's vocabulary through his pupils resulted in the creation of a great many centrally-planned buildings that remodelled that of St Peter's Basilica, albeit on a smaller scale.

Private palaces and civilian buildings

Generally speaking, up to the early quattrocento, residential building evolved only marginally compared with the development of religious buildings and public edifices. Architectural studies focused on defining and perfecting models for public buildings, which were considered to be representative of communities. Churches, (as well as the basilica typology), bathhouses and theatres took on clearly defined forms that were honed over time, while the private nature of residential buildings meant that there were no basic examples to replicate and thus the typology evolved naturally in response to practical requirements. However, from the Middle Ages onwards, several events served to destroy the dichotomy between high architecture and residential architec-

Antonio da Sangallo the Younger, Courtyard of Palazzo Farnese, from 1514, Rome (left) and the Colosseum, 80 AD, Rome (right)

The Renaissance predilection for antique models is also evident in the façade configurations of the buildings, which feature the superimposition of classical orders typical of Roman buildings. The Colosseum, characterised by its rising succession of Tuscan, Ionic and Corinthian orders became the inspiration for the courtyard of Palazzo Farnese. The construction of the palazzo was started by the architect, Antonio da Sangallo the Younger in 1515, whilst the upper level was completed by Michelangelo in 1534. The building reproduced the vertical articulation of the antique amphitheatre's three classical orders.

ture. This took place when both approaches were amalgamated to produce the fortified castle, often based on a symmetrical plan, which indicated the characteristic traits that future developments would take.

The desire to subject civilian building to a planning process that regularised its constituent parts was evident as early as the Tuscan Proto-Renaissance. Palazzo Vecchio, built during the first half of the 14th century, represents the first attempt to organise the façade into regular spaces. It was during the early 15th century, however, with the rediscovery of the Antique and the use of the Antique Roman lexicon, that a significant shift took place. The revolutionary change of style also applied to residential building, triggering lofty alterations to housing models. The increasing attention paid by architects to residences aimed to imbue residential homes with a new architectural dignity, achieved by regularising the components of the plan and elevation and adopting the new *all'antica* style. Florentine economic power rested in the hands of an oligarchy of rich merchants whose desire for social acceptance provided the perfect context for the dissemination of the new architecture in private palazzi. Palazzo Medici, designed for Cosimo I by the architect, Michelozzo in 1444, was the first of the new residences to be built in Florence for the newly established patrons and became the benchmark for residential buildings to follow. From the outset, the theoretical point of reference was Roman habitation described by Vitruvius in his treaty; this showed configurations according to an axial layout in which three spaces: *vestibulum, atrium*

Palagio di Parte Guelfa, 14th century, Florence

The extent of Brunelleschi's contribution to the 14th century Palagio di Parte Guelfa remains disputed, both in terms of chronology and of œuvre. What is certain, however, is that he enhanced the top part of the façade by adding a few simple elements, such as the generous windows surmounted by oculi and the tall pilasters, which were to demarkate the corners of the building. These were, unfortunately never completed and only a mere trace of them remains today.

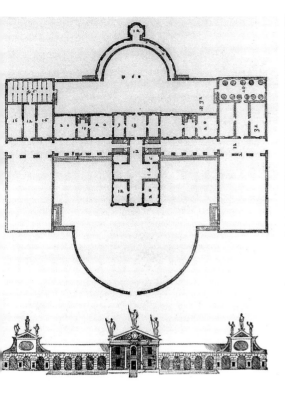

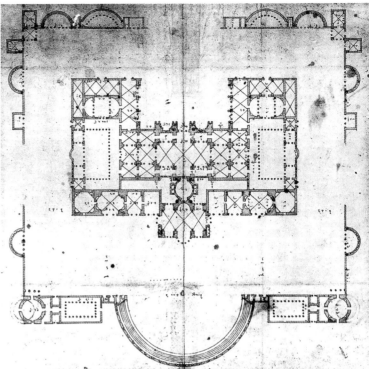

and *peristylium*, proceeding one another. The colonnaded courtyard was to form the private heart of the ancient habitation surrounded by various rooms organised symmetrically. The vitruvian system was to remain the basic model for residential buildings throughout the Renaissance, with an infinite variety of interpretations and reconstructions. The use of orders for regulating façades seems to have made its first appearance in Brunelleschi's design for the Palagio di Parte Guelfa in 1435 and was perfected a dozen or so years later formally by Alberti in Palazzo Rucellai, where the superimposition of the orders, as in ancient theatres, became the norm in the designs of elevations. However, the articulation of façades by means of architectural orders failed to gain popularity in Medici Florence and later buildings, such as Palazzo Strozzi, were variations on the theme of Palazzo Medici, featuring massive blocks of rusticated stone and protruding cornices. Experimenting with plans based on Antique models continued throughout the 15th century; houses built around a central courtyard even became the basis for complex designs featuring a large number of buildings and several courtyards, as in Giuliano da Sangallo's monumental design for a the Medici Palace in Florence. The spatial expansion of buildings became a set feature in the design of Roman villas during both the early and late cinquecento, and found its purest expression in the work of Palladio, who gained new stimuli and developed new prototypes from his study of Antiquity.

Andrea Palladio, Plan and elevation of Villa Barbaro at Maser, Viterbo *The Four Books of Architecture*, Venice 1570 (left) and Andrea Palladio, geometric study of the Diocletian Baths in Rome, London, Royal Institute of British Architects, SBI34/v/i (right)

The monumentality of Palladio's architecture and the layouts of his residences in the Venetian hinterland, in particular the imperial baths which reinterpret the typology of antique architecture — a complex and grandiose succession of symmetrical spaces comprising a model that Palladio altered according to the desires of his patrons.
The symmetrical scheme, characterised by a communal nucleus with wings and a convex volume in the centre, surrounded by an enclosure with exedra, is drawn from the Diocletian Baths, which Palladio would undoubtedly have studied.

THE QUATTROCENTO

From the early quattrocento onwards, the formal revival of classical architecture and the rediscovery of the ruins of Imperial Rome became increasingly systematic and exacting: the baths, the basilicas and the ancient temples all became points of reference in the formulation of a new language that owed its illustrious and noble origins to the Antique.

Brunelleschi's revolutionary spatial structuring was the catalyst for the humanist architects' discovery of ancient architecture as the ideal aesthetic point of reference, both in terms of plan layout and of elevational design. Field studies of the Roman ruins formed an obligatory part of the professional training of architects, which led to the birth of a new literary genre that consisted of illustrated guides to the antiquities, which helped to disseminate the basic prototypes. Advances in measuring techniques, together with the fact that many artists were extremely adept at duplicating, meant that a huge corpus of drawings was produced, which to this day constitutes the most concrete proof of the great influence the Antique had on the architecture of the Renaissance.

Through comparison and analysis of ancient remains with the treaty on architecture written by Vitruvius during the 1st century BC philological architectural developments increasingly comprised classical pieces. The existence of the treaty was already recognised during medieval times — although it was not published until 1486 by Sulpicio da Veroli — an archaelogist at the Accademia Romana during Innocent VIII's papacy. The treaty was dedicated to Marcus Vitruvius Pollione, an architect/engineer, who lead Caesar's artillery. Vitruvius served as an architect under Emperor Augustus.

Leon Battista Alberti, Detail of the
façade of Sant'Andrea, 1472, Mantua

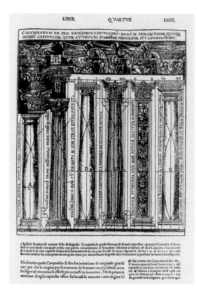 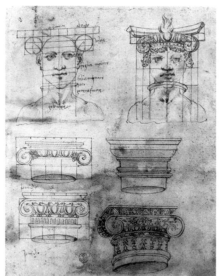

left
Cesare Cesariano, Presentation of various orders of columns and capitals, from Vitruvius, *De Architectura*, **1521, Como, vol. LXIIIr**

The original version of Vitruvius's treaty was devoid of illustrations, but so great was the interest in his work during the Renaissance that numerous editions were published from the late 15th century onwards. The translation of the treaty by Cesariano, a Milanese painter and pupil of Bramante during the reign of Ludovico Sforza, is full of his sketched reconstructions of the typologies and details described by Vitruvius.

right
Francesco di Giorgio Martini, Anthropomorphical capitals, Turin, Biblioteca Reale, Codex Saluzziano 148, XXI.4, vol. 15r

Francesco di Giorgio found Vitruvius's anthropomorphical theories deeply fascinating. Di Giorgio devoted a great deal of space to the analogies between architecture and the human body in the illustrations in his treaty on civil and military architecture. A recurring theme is the proportion of the human head as the measurement for capitals, which forms part of the theory as to why the various shapes of columns correspond to different types of human figures. Di Giorgio's studies extended beyond Vitruvius's treaty, postulating even more corresponding aspects, such as the base of columns to human feet, dentils to teeth, in a highly imaginative concept of the design process.

Not a great deal is known about the architectural work of Vitruvius, apart, perhaps, from the now-ruined basilica at Fano. Vitruvius's treaty, which is obscure in places and which was initially published without illustrations, became the springboard for free figurative drawings of Roman architecture. These frequently depicted reconstructions based on inadequate examples due to the complexity of the text or the lack of suitable building types on which architects could base new, modern buildings for their clients. Following the first print-run of Vitruvius's treaty it was republished many times, often with plates produced by the editors: the first illustrated edition by Fra' Giocondo was published in 1511, whilst Cesare Cesariano's Italian translation was published in Como in 1521.

Leon Battista Alberti, one of the quattrocento's most eclectic and influential characters, wrote the first Renaissance architectural treatise, the *De Re Aedificatoria* (*Ten Books on Architecture*), which was published in 1485. The treatise is structured faithfully according to Vitruvius; though Alberti researched his sources more thoroughly. Although Vitruvius remained his preferred point of reference, Alberti also studied many other ancient texts — many of which have now been lost — and devoted himself to the on-site study of Roman ruins. Alberti's concept of beauty, which has its foundation in Vitruvius's writings on aesthetics, is based on the harmony of the elements and the optimal proportions for any particular component — capital, edifice or city — ensuring that nothing could be removed without jeopardising its perfection (*concinnitas*). Beauty was, therefore, closely tied to the symmetry and proportion of the different elements as well as to the human figure — regarded as the greatest source of harmonious proportions created by Nature — became the golden rule for measurements. The belief that the visible world could be ordered by mathematical reasoning is typical of Renaissance humanist thinking and led to the definition of perspective as the means by which this could be achieved in spatial terms.

The Florentine architect, Antonio Averulino, known as Filarete, produced a treaty in the form of a dialogue, which he dedicated to Francesco Sforza. Filarete incites the latter to abandon the "appalling Gothic style" introduced into Italy by "barbarous" people and to turn instead to the "ancient way of building" in the manner of Brunelleschi in Florence. Filarete's primary influence was also Vitruvius and despite the fact that the content of the treaty was completely at odds with the precision and lucidity of Alberti's œuvre, it nevertheless revealed that Filarete was acquainted with *De re aedificatoria*. Filarete describes the ideal city in detail, which he symbolically names Sforzinda, where various principles of Alberti, such as centrality, order and symmetry recur. The text is embellished with highly imaginative and scenic drawings which illustrate some of the most important buildings of the city, as well as some of Alberti's own buildings.

Various versions of the anthropomorphical principles behind the Vitruvian theories are illustrated in the treaty on civil and military architecture written in Urbino by Sienese architect, Francesco di Giorgio Martini (1439–1501) in around 1480. Martini's treaty provides one of the clearest first-hand accounts of Renaissance iconography and deals with architecture in its broadest and most general sense: from military techniques to typological studies into ancient architecture, from cities down to decorative detail. This universality of knowledge was something that struck a chord with both Martini and da Vinci, the writings of whom are well known, despite the fact that they were never compiled in the form of a treaty. The two architects were well acquainted with one another; there is documentary evidence that da Vinci's library contained a copy of Martini's treaty, which was apparently well thumbed and scrupulously annotated.

Architectural theory of the 15th century, whilst attempting a prescriptive method, also reflected the humanist and anthropocentric concept of the early Renaissance by reformulating ancient vocabulary in a quest for aesthetic and cultural perfection. By the close of the century, however, this Utopian vision and the concept of the ideal city as a reflection of a perfect civilisation were already being jeopardised by the new political and social scenarios and, therefore, ceased to be feasible.

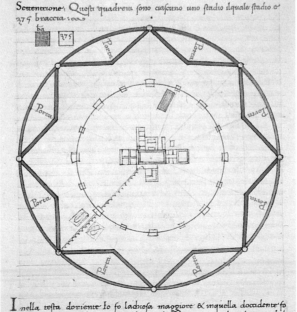

Antonio Averlino known as Filarete, Plan for the idea city of Sforzinda, 1462–1464, Florence, Biblioteca Nazionale Centrale, Codex Magliabechi II, 1, 140, vol. 43r

Filarete's architectural treaty, drawn up in the early 1460s, was first dedicated to Francesco Sforza and then to Piero de' Medici; it contains the description of the ideal eight-point star-shaped imaginary city of Sforzinda. Filarete's aim was an attempt to define a Utopian vision of a city, in which the symmetrical, concentric layout of the streets tied in symbolically with Vitruvius's geometric theories.

THE RENAISSANCE PERIOD

The mathematical and geometrical theories that underpinned the spatial renewal of the early quattrocento owed a great deal to the discovery of perspective as a means of three-dimensional representation. According to both Filarete and the biographer, Manetti, it was Brunelleschi who revolutionised figurative illustration during the 1420s, scientifically proving his theory by means of two small paintings which both depicted Florentine urban landscapes, namely the Baptistery as seen from the door of the Duomo and the Piazza della Signoria. The paintings were not supposed to be regarded straight on, but rather from behind through a hole where the image was reflected in a mirror. This device demonstrated that the convergence of orthog-

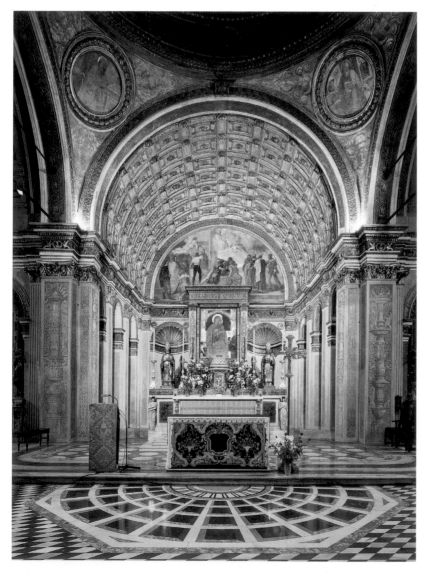

Bramante, Perspective of the choir, Santa Maria adjacent to San Satiro, 1482, Milan

Bramante's presence in the builders' yard at the Milanese church of San Satiro is documented from 1482 onwards. Santa Maria was built to a basilica plan and derives directly from Brunelleschi's layout for Santo Spirito. The church was embedded into the city's dense urban fabric; this meant that there was no space for Bramante to include the broad, centric space below the cupola that had become the principal characteristic of Renaissance churches from Brunelleschi's time. Bramante's solution was to create a trompe l'œil stucco and gilded bas relief of a chancel with truncated barrel-vaulted ceiling supported by lateral piers, that created the optical illusion of a fourth arm of the Latin cross.

Masaccio, Holy Trinity, Santa Maria Novella, 1426–1428, Florence and perspectival view (below)

Masaccio's fresco is an early illustration of Brunelleschi's principles of perspective. The scene is a majestic and ancient one, in which two Corinthian pilasters support a classical entablature and frame an overtly foreshortened, coffered barrel-vaulted ceiling designed to give an illusion of depth. The orthogonals converge at a point where the two patrons of the work are kneeling, composed to draw in the spectator's eye. Man is clearly the primary protagonist here. The architectural format of the painting — apparently the art of perspective was taught to him by his friend, Masaccio and Brunelleschi may well have been involved himself in its creation — is underscored by the duotone structures, the skilful precision and the extremely fine detail.

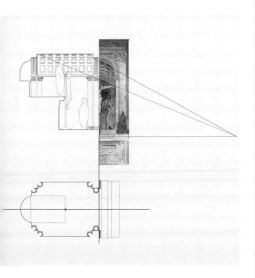

Interior, Santo Spirito, Florence, showing modular and proportional details of the plan

The design for Santo Spirito rests on a modular scheme that regulates and determines the measurements and proportions of the building as an entirety. Simply by multiplying the intervals between the eleven *braccia* columns all the principal building measurements can be calculated. The volumetric ratios between the parts based on the elementary cube form create a harmonious whole and serve to demonstrate Brunelleschi's loyalty to the ideal vitruvian *concinnitas*.

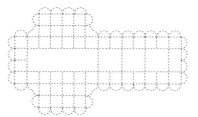
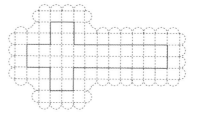

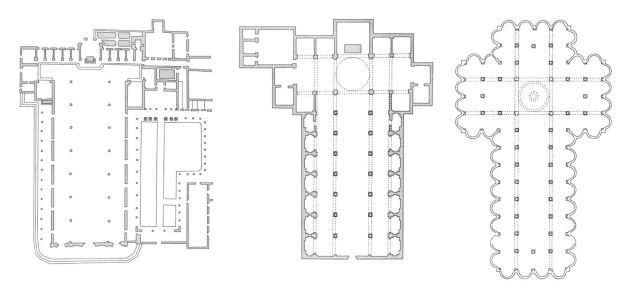

onal lines could be determined via a focal point, which served to reduce the size of volumes nearest to the focal point. Brunelleschi's discovery was fundamental to Renaissance art and had a profound effect on representation: the concept of the world and nature ceased to be objective, over and above man, but became subjective, with the human eye as the ultimate visual apparatus. The rules of perspective, on which Renaissance anthropocentrism was founded, quickly disseminated around 15th century Florence and became a focus for artistic debate several decades later in the courts of Federico da Montefeltro in Urbino, which was a hotbed of mathematical scholars and painters at that time. The scientific texts written by Piero della Francesca and Luca Pacioli in Urbino are proof of the tremendous humanist interest in mathematical and proportional principles and spawned a new figurative ideal where the intellect reigned supreme.

From the 15th century onwards, the approach to the art of architecture underwent a seismic change. The medieval practice of design and building processes progressed simultaneously and was overtaken by a compositional logic where the overall plan for buildings preceded and guided their realisation. Renaissance architects used methods of drawing to explore all possible solutions with regard to typology and form, adhering to a series of established geometric and proportional rules. The Renaissance concept of space was highly indebted to the study of Vitruvius's mathematical and proportional theories and to Roman antiquities in general. Mathematical reflection became the intellectual instrument for the architectural composition of buildings, which started to be designed using a new, graphic, technical language. Plans, sections and elevations were drawn up according to simple rules, based on modular reproduction and the symmetrical alignment of parts of the plan and the overall building volumes. This compositional process, pioneered by Brunelleschi, led to the creation of increasingly centralised spaces, characterised by the juxtaposition of elementary solids, parallelogramms, cubes, cylinders and half spheres, with cupolas providing the logical volumetric enclosure. The evolution of formal planning research was to culminate during the 16th century in a few highly complex, multi-axial buildings, articulated along various symmetrical axes.

Brunelleschi's original plans for Santa Croce (left), San Lorenzo (centre) and Santo Spirito (right), Florence

The traditional plan layout of 13th century monastic churches featured a nave, a transept and a choir. This layout was utilised during the Renaissance by Brunelleschi in the church of San Lorenzo and perfected in his design for Santo Spirito. The confident design and unhomogeneous proportions of the medieval spaces gave way to the unprecedented compositional clarity of Brunelleschi's architecture. His deep intellectual allegiance to humanist principles culminated in the creation of a central space characterised by the perfect axial symmetry of the parts. The original design for Santo Spirito, which, alas, never came to fruition, also provided for the continuation of the semicircular chapels on the entrance side of the building.

THE MASTERPIECE
THE CUPOLA OF SANTA MARIA DEL FIORE IN FLORENCE

In 1418 the Arte della Lana (Guild of Wool Merchants), who were responsible for ecumenical works, held a competition for building the cupola of Santa Maria del Fiore.

Designed by Arnolfo, the Duomo was first modified by Francesco Talenti, who extended the plan in 1360. The design was later altered by Giovanni di Lapo Ghini during the late 14th century. Ghini built an octagonal drum, 13 metres high above the aisles as an impost for the cupola. This resulted in an enormous space, measuring over 41 metres in height — only fractionally lower than the upper limit permitted for masonry domes of this type.

Brunelleschi, who was in charge of the builders' yard that opened on August 7, 1420, came up with an ingenious solution to the problem. His scheme managed to avoid the use of expensive timbers, which would, in any case, probably have proved impracticable for work on this scale. Brunelleschi designed a dome that would be self-supporting at each stage of construction and that — despite its formal Gothic appearance, with a pointed vault and ribs demarkating the sections — would behave structurally like a semi-spherical vault supported by consecutive rings, (similar to the Pantheon in Rome). This feat of engineering greatly influenced the new baths which Renaissance architecture was navigating. Brunelleschi was no longer regarded as just any builder, but rather gained recognition as the master architect who had conceived the plan, organising every stage of the construction process, from the design to the models to the practical building methods, taking total responsibility for the project. This also included dealing with the labourers. The completion of the cupola, which his contemporaries duly recognised as an extraordinary achievement, should not overshadow the formal aspects of the building that was to change the face of Florence forever. It is impossible to walk along the 14th century nave and not be awestruck by the great central space that opens out in the tribune area, the volumetric and spiritual heart of the building.

Filippo Brunelleschi, Cupola of Santa Maria del Fiore, 1420–1436, Florence

The exterior of the cupola is articulated by eight large, pale marble ribs that converge at the centre in an octagon, standing out formally and chromatically against the russet tiles, producing a strong contrasting effect that can be clearly evident even when viewed from afar. The bulk of Brunelleschi's dome stands proud of the city fabric to become a focal point for anyone looking down on Florence from the surrounding hills, creating an integral part of Florence's urban landscape.

The enduring civic value of the construction was immediately understood by Alberti who dedicated his *De Pictura* to Brunelleschi in 1436, where he describes the cupola as "ample, capable of enveloping all the Tuscan peoples in its shadow."

Structure of the cupola of Santa Maria del Fiore, 1420–1436, Florence

The cupola of Santa Maria del Fiore is made up of two shells: a heavier, load-bearing inner shell and a lighter, protective outer shell "to protect it from damp, and to make it look more magnificent and inflated," as communicated in the stipulations of July 1420. The masonry that creates the façade of the eight sections was laid in a herringbone pattern, in order to prevent the weight from simply shifting vertically downwards, distributing it in several different directions, thus making the structure as a whole more structurally sound. Brunelleschi's approach to structural problems stood side by side with the practical challenges of building construction. Thus, Brunelleschi designed and developed several machines — real feats of engineering — with which to lift the huge loads of materials to great heights. This made an enormous difference to the labour, cutting down on both time and cost.

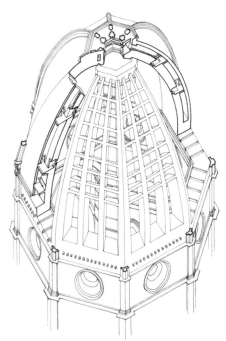

THE URBAN FLORENTINE PALACE

The ascent of a new secular political class, composed of merchants and bankers, triggered the wave of urban renewal that was to flood so many Italian cities, but Florence primarily. The need for grand residences that flaunted social status, together with the significant investment opportunities, led to a new style of urban villa, where the rationalisation of spaces was guided by the rediscovery of the classical vocabulary. The compositional rules for building Florence's new urban palazzo were derived directly from Vitruvius's treaty and his descriptions of the houses built during Antiquity, which provided the prototypical model for Renaissance residences. Symmetry of plan layout, with spaces arranged around a colonnaded courtyard and symmetrical façades, often articulated by superimposed architectural orders, were the golden rules that informed the building of urban residences from 15th century Florence right up to the time of Palladio and beyond. The application of the Vitruvian code to orders in residential buildings seems to have been adopted at an early stage by Brunelleschi, who, already in 1435, clad the exterior of the Palagio di Parte Guelfa with unusual gigantic pilasters. During this period, Brunelleschi submitted a design to Cosimo il Vecchio for a large palazzo near to the church of San Lorenzo. His design was rejected as being too ornate and the commission was awarded to Michelozzo.

opposite page
Leon Battista Alberti, Detail from the façade of Palazzo Rucellai, 1453, Florence

The palace built for Giovanni Rucellai was achieved by integrating various structures, remodelled around a new central courtyard, with a new stone façade, in front of which a square and a communal family loggia were built at Rucellai's behest. Alberti is thought to have commenced work on the façade — conceived independently from the internal works — in 1453. The design, which features three storeys of decreasing height each separated by a string course was designed in the Florentine tradition, as was its precedent, Palazzo Medici, built a few years earlier. Palazzo Rucellai was built to the same composition, although on a smaller scale. The most remarkable thing about Alberti's palazzo was his use of classical orders to structure the façade, which is surmounted by pilasters of different orders, articulating the horizontal intervals between the windows. The idea was to revolutionise domestic residences and was clearly derived from models of Roman architecture, the Colosseum in particular, which Alberti cited precisely, down to even the smallest details such as the absence of metopes and triglyphs in the frieze of the Doric order and the brackets supporting the upper corinthian cornice contained in the lower frieze.

Michelozzo, view from Palazzo Medici Riccardi, 1444, Florence

Building began on the huge palazzo in Via Larga in 1444 according to a design by Michelozzo, the Medici family architect. The exterior of the building follows the tradition of medieval Florentine palazzi such as Palazzo Vecchio; its fortified character, typical of 14th century buildings, was accentuated by the rusticated stone on the ground floor plinth.
The wall mass diminishes in the upper floors, culminating in a large *all'antica* modillion cornice, which emphasises the great geometric volume of the palazzo as it rises from the complex city fabric.

LEON BATTISTA ALBERTI

Leon Battista Alberti was born in 1404 into a Florentine family exiled in Genoa; he studied canon and civil law at Bologna University but it was not until 1428, when the ban against his family was eventually lifted that he was able to return to Florence. Alberti was a quintessential Renaissance man exerting enormous influence in many different artistic fields. He was literary, a philosopher, an art theorist and architect; and left writings of unparalleled intellectual clarity in each of these spheres and which informed the continuous cross-pollination of the various disciplines. The *De Statua* and *De Pictura*, along with the *Della Famiglia* volumes, are a testament to the vast range of his interests. These publications were followed by his most important work, *De Re Aedificatoria*, the architectural treaty that was correctly regarded as *the* humanist manifesto. His extensive cultural breadth and his considerable experience took him to various Italian courts and cities, which meant that he was the ultimate embodiment of the intellectual Renaissance humanist. Alberti's architectural career and his prestigious role as Papal Advisor took him to various places, enabling him to travel widely with the papal court. Alberti renovated Sigismondo Malatesta's dynastic temple in Rimini in 1450 and is then thought to have been involved in Pope Nicholas V's ambitious urban remodelling plan for Rome. It was to Pope Nicholas V that Alberti dedicated his 1452 treaty. During the 1450s and 1460s the architect was commissioned to design various buildings in Florence by Giovanni Rucellai. Subsequently, between 1460 and 1472, the year in which Alberti died, he realised the project designed for Ludovico Gonzaga, Marquis of Mantua.

Leon Battista Alberti, San Sebastiano, begun 1460, Mantua

The church of San Sebastiano, in Mantua, begun in 1460, is built according to a central plan. San Sebastiano was the first Renaissance church to be built in the Greek cross plan format, which was to be repeated several times over the coming years, firstly by Giuliano da Sangallo at Santa Maria delle Carceri in Prato. The short, coffered arms were probably supposed to have terminated at the centre of a cupola, however this was never built. The exterior of the building, accessed from a raised step, resembles the pronaos of a classical temple, with a tympanum at the apex, now broken, which appears to feature the same motif as that of the Roman triumphal arch in Orange.

Leon Battista Alberti, San Francesco, 1450, Rimini (above) and Matteo de' Pasti, Commemorative medal depicting Alberti's original design (right)

The church of San Francesco in Rimini was the burial place for the local nobility from the early trecento onwards, but it was Sigismondo Pandolfo Malatesta who set about transforming the old church into a dynastic temple that proclaimed the glory and repute of the patron family. Alberti started work on the church in 1450 and built a series of arcades in istrian stone supported on a continuous base, drawn directly from Roman monuments. The revival of ancient motifs is even more obvious in the façade, the original design of which

featured on the commemorative medal attributed to Matteo de' Pasti. The lower portion of the building, articulated by three arcades, derives directly from the Arch of Augustus in Rimini and is clearly intended to draw a comparison between Sigismondo and the triumphant Roman emperor. The two lateral arcades, later demolished, were intended to house the sepulchre of Malatesta and his wife, Isotta, in a scheme reminiscent of an ancient mausoleum; the great cupola in the middle of the transept also recalls an ancient mausoleum. The cupola features on the medal but was unfortunately never realised.

IOHANES ORICELLARIVS PAV F AN SAL MCCCCLXX

left
Leon Battista Alberti, Santa Maria Novella, 1458–1460, Florence

Alberti's design for the façade of Santa Maria Novella, informed by his earlier work on the Tempio Malatestiano, was harmoniously symmetrical, incorporating the pre-existing medieval decoration on the lower part of the façade into a classical scheme.

The arched orders framing the portal are offset by the tall piers that demarkate the corners and are surmounted by a high attic, which solved some of the incongruities that had remained unresolved in the building and facilitated the transition from the small scale medieval ornamentation to the large squares in the upper part. The two sections of the façade are brought together by two large volutes, which tie in chromatically with the rest of the elevations. The entire façade is inscribed within a square.

Leon Battista Alberti, Rucellai Chapel, 1460s, San Pancrazio, Florence

In the 1460s Giovanni Rucellai commissioned Alberti to remodel a small chapel in the church of San Pancrazio near the palazzo in Via della Vigna. The chapel was intended to house Rucellai's sepulchre, which was to replicate the Shrine of the Holy Sepulchre in Jerusalem, familiar already during the quattrocento from descriptions brought back to Europe by pilgrims from the Holy Land. The chromatic and decorative simplicity of the chapel — which was a clear reference to Brunelleschi's recently completed Pazzi Chapel — is offset by the decorative sophistication of the small rectangular sepulchre, finished with marble inlay and surmounted by a lantern with a small spiral cupola. The fine antique-style inscription in Roman script comes to the fore among the intricate geometric patterns.

THE MASTERPIECE
SANT'ANDREA IN MANTUA

The Council convened by Pope Pius remained at the Court of Ludovico Gonzaga, Marquis of Mantua, from mid 1459 to early 1460. Alberti accompanied the papal court on this occasion and grew close to the Gonzaga family, for whom he was to later build the churches of San Sebastiano and Sant'Andrea.

Sant'Andrea was a Benedictine abbey situated in the heart of Mantua, which Ludovico had, for some time, wanted to rebuild in a more modern fashion, as a more fitting addition to the city.

The correspondence between Alberti and his patron indicate that Ludovico wanted a generous church, with no visual obstacles in the nave that might impede the congregation's view of the Blood of Christ, the most sacred aspect of the liturgy in Mantua.

Gonzaga's ambitious designs were, however, never realised due to the Abbot's staunch opposition to the demolition of the medieval building. The Abbot died in 1470 and two years later the ancient church was demolished in order to make room for a new one. Unfortunately, Alberti died during the spring of that year and so the building was completed by Luca Fancelli. Despite later interventions that altered the original appearance of the building, the Basilica of Sant'Andrea remains one of the formative buildings of the Renaissance and an exemplary example of Alberti's interpretation of Roman architecture.

opposite page
Leon Battista Alberti,
Sant'Andrea, 1472, Mantua

The floor plan for Sant'Andrea is characterised by a long single nave covered with a barrel vault and culminating in a small transept covered by a central cupola in a basilica scheme. The configuration of the exterior is the culmination of Alberti's research into façades. As in both other projects, the Tempio Malatestiano and Santa Maria Novella, Alberti was endeavouring to bring two classical systems together: the triumphal arch and the temple pronaos. The triumphal arch on the façade of Sant'Andrea has a single high, narrow opening — as in Titus's Arch in Rome and the Trajan Arch in Ancona — and features an entablature that extends into the two blind side bays. The entablature is surmounted by four tall piers supporting a heavy classical gable, thus enabling the two systems to intersect harmoniously. Alberti's fusion of two systems was to formalise a typology that became fundamental to the evolution of architecture and was to be perfected by Palladio almost a century later.

Leon Battista Alberti, Plan and
nave of Sant'Andrea, 1472, Mantua

The majestic nave in Sant'Andrea features a powerful coffered barrel-vaulted ceiling that allows the building to be classed as 'ancient.' The nave is flanked by alternating open and closed side chapels: the larger open chapels are also covered with barrel vaults, while the smaller spaces contain hollow forms that act as buttresses to the vault. The system of lateral spaces is articulated by arch orders that frame the openings and confer a rhythmic pattern that was to become extremely popular.
The tall pilasters framing the chapels are repeated in the dividing walls of the closed spaces, making room for classical portals surmounted by oculi. The width of the barrel vault over the nave and the structure of the side chapels that open out into the great piers resonate with unusual Roman gravitas, reminiscent of the Massenzio Basilica, which Alberti may have been referring to in a letter to Ludovico, when he describes the Etruscan temple as being the best shape for the edifice.

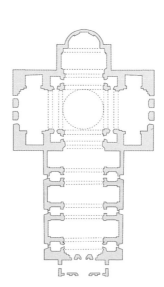

ARCHITECTURAL RENEWAL IN MILAN

By the middle of the quattrocento, Milan's builders' yards were still being organised in a medieval manner. The dominant figures were the engineers and supervisors who were traditionally dependent on the extended Solari family, who had influenced all Lombard achievements of any significance. A new approach to architecture began to take hold from 1450 when Francesco Sforza came to power. Sforza, a famous *condottiero* and consummate politician, married the daughter of Filippo Maria Visconti, ushering in a period of peace and financial prosperity. Sforza commissioned new civil and religious buildings and through his financial and diplomatic links with the Medici family contrived to enlighten the conservative Milanese to the artistic renewal taking place in central Italy. Sforza summoned the Florentine architect, Antonio Averlino, known as Filarete, to Milan and commissioned him with building the façade of the Castle as well as a new hospital, which was begun in 1456. Between 1460 and 1464, Filarete worked on a treaty which he initially dedicated to the Duke of Milan and later, on his return to Florence after 1465, to Piero de' Medici. In his treaty, Filarete describes the imaginary city of Sforzinda, providing drawings of real and imaginary buildings to illustrate his elucidations. Thanks to Sforza's connections in the city of Florence, Filarete was also commissioned to build two projects for Pigello Portinari, a financier of the Medici family in Milan. These projects were the Banco Mediceo, which is also featured in the treaty (only the portal remains today) and the Portinari Chapel in the church of Sant'Eustorgio which was designed as a mausoleum for Portinari, who died in 1468.

Filarete (?), Portinari Chapel,
Sant'Eustorgio, begun 1462, Milan

Building work on this small chapel — frequently attributed to Filarete — began in 1462.
The chapel was commissioned by Pigello Portinari, the Medici financial representative in Milan. The plan layout of the chapel clearly derives from the Old Sacristy in Florence, a building that had particular significance for Pigello Portinari by virtue of being the Medici family sepulchre. The Brunelleschi-inspired scheme was reformulated in a particularly Lombardy style, evident in the lavish pictorial interior decoration as well as the configuration of the exterior, with its high hexadecagonal lantern.

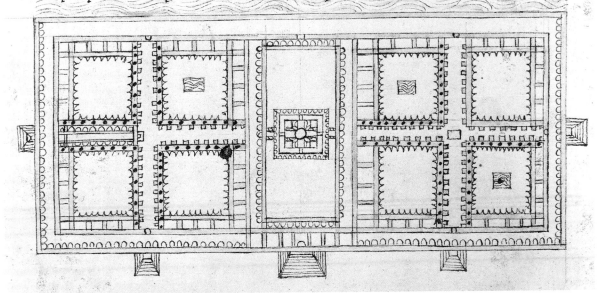

crifiquo atacchare & ancora laporta delmezzo alentrata delchiostro:
n lachiefa feci una porta dimarmo laquale dunano fuo era bra aque

THE IDEAL CITY

Whereas during the first half of the quattrocento the architectural revival of classical canons was largely confined to Florence, during the second half of the century they began to take hold elsewhere in Italy where the regional provinces were prospering. The princely courts, with cultivated and energetic patrons in their leadership, became centres for intellectual and formal research, attracting a large number of architects who were summoned to collaborate in the renovation projects. Federico da Montefeltro in Urbino, Pandolfo Malatesta in Rimini, the Este family in Ferrara and the Gonzaga family in Mantua and especially the Medici family — who ruled over Florence continuously from 1434 to 1494 — were promoters of large-scale initiatives. The trend towards symmetry and modularity, so characteristic of Renaissance architecture, soon began to shape urban design, informing plans for orderly rectilinear layouts and broad urban squares. The guidelines for the ideal city were described by Alberti in his *De Re Aedificatoria*, which soon became an aesthetic and ideological credo for the Renaissance princes, with ancient cities regarded as the ideal models to emulate. The spatial and programmatic rigour applied to building the new settlements, such as Pienza, failed to take hold and was superseded by a desire to insert all new buildings sensitively into the existing medieval urban fabric.

opposite page
Francesco di Giorgio Martini, Human figure superimposed onto the plan for a small citadel, Turin, Biblioteca Reale, Codex Saluzziano

The loyalty of Renaissance architects to the principles of anthropomorphic harmony drawn from Vitruvius's treaty was also extended to Vitruvius's theories on the ideal city. As this drawing by Francesco di Giorgio illustrates, the human figure constitutes the perfect form for a fortified citadel where the head corresponds to the fortress, the limbs to the great towers and the chest to the square overlooked by the temple — the true heart of the city.

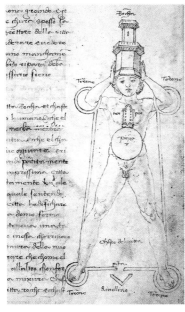

Central Italian Artist. The Ideal City, late 15th century, Urbino, Galleria Nazionale delle Marche

The Renaissance fascination with the city is illustrated by three oil paintings of urban *vedute* conserved in museums in Baltimore, Berlin and Urbino. The vedute are timber panels, made to tie in with a decorative scheme or a wall, in the tradition of the inlaid perspectives so popular in Urbino circles at that time. The Urbino painting shows the wings of two classical buildings framing a square, in the centre of which stands a circular temple articulated by columns. The configuration of the buildings, which appear to be drawn precisely from some of Alberti's architecture and the shape of the square, which is drawn from the passages in *De Re Aedificatoria* on the ideal city and its perfect temple have caused many scholars to attribute the building to Alberti. This theory is backed by the recent discovery of a beautifully-finished drawing beneath the painted surface.

THE MASTERPIECE
PIENZA

On his way to Mantua to a religious council in 1459, Pope Pius II Piccolomini siezed the opportunity to visit his native village of Corsignano, a small medieval settlement on the crest of a hill overlooking the Val d'Orcia. Within a short space of time, the Pontiff decided to transform Corsignano into a memorial city, rename it Pienza and dedicate it to his influential family. The Piccolomini family had already consolidated its political and financial power in Sienna by building several prestigious buildings. Pope Pius was a cultivated and well-informed humanist, just as deeply devoted to the study of classical literature and Roman antiquities as to modern trends; he was also an ambitious patron. Pius was accompanied by Alberti on his journey to Mantua. Alberti is thought to have suggested a master plan for the urban remodelling of the village according to the principles outlined in his treaty — though this is not documented. The Florentine architect, Bernardo Rossellino, then at the height of his professional ca-

reer, was commissioned to realise the design. Rossellino was later appointed Supervisor of Santa Maria del Fiore, in 1461. The architect's plan included the central part of the village, providing for the construction of a trapezoidal-shaped square in an area overlooking the valley, which was surrounded by the church, the Palazzo Piccolomini, the bishop's residence and the Palazzo Comunale. The village was renamed Pienza in 1462, becoming the first example of the ideal Utopian Renaissance city.

The cathedral was designed according to an example Pius had seen in Austria and which he hoped to reproduce here; it was divided into three aisles of equal height. The cathedral acted as a backdrop to the square and partially screened the view of the valley beyond. The neighbouring buildings were part of the general plan; they were inserted sideways along two oblique axes that extended into two openings overlooking the green hills of the Val d'Orcia.

bottom, left
View of the Piazza di Pienza, Sienna

The artist's adherence to Alberti's principles is clear from the central focus of the temple volume as well as in the configuration of the church façade, with its motif of the triumphal arch framed by classical orders. Palazzo Piccolomini, adjacent to the church, is built in the classical style typical of Florentine palazzi of the time. The palazzo has a colonnaded courtyard at the centre, whilst the exterior is adorned with superimposed orders that articulate the apertures in a similar fashion to Palazzo Rucellai built a few years earlier by Alberti and which was the inspirational model for Rossellini's designs.

Plan of the Piazza di Pienza, Sienna

The square opens on to the cathedral façade (3), with Palazzo Piccolomini on the right (1).
An elegant well-curb (2) sits above two circular steps alongside the palace.

THE MASTERPIECE
THE DUCAL PALACE IN URBINO

The death of Guidantonio da Montefeltro in 1443, closely followed by that of his legitimate heir Oddantonio, enabled his other son, Federico, to take over power to becoming one of the most enlightened of the Renaissance patrons. During Federico da Montefeltro's lengthy rule, from 1444 to 1482, great artists such as Alberti, who dedicated his treatise, *De Re Aedificatoria*, to Federico, passed through the courts of Urbino. Architects such as Francesco Laurana, Francesco di Giorgio, Baccio Pontelli and Giuliano da Maiano as well as artists such as Piero della Francesca, Pedro Berruguete, Giusto di Gand and Melozzo da Forlì all worked on the ambitious renovation project for Federico's palace and the city as a whole. It was in this enlightened and cosmopolitan atmosphere, which survived even after Federico's death, that Bramante received his training in perspectival representation from Fra' Carnevale and Piero della Francesca. The Duke seemed to have driven the complex renovation project himself, which meant organising and coordinating a great many different tasks. He was an extremely cultivated man, who had been educated by the learned humanist Vittorino da Feltre; said to have been an amateur architect himself.

Building is likely to have started on the palace during the early 1460s, apparently to a design by the Dalmatian architect, Luciano Laurana, who completed the model of the edifice in Mantua in 1466. Two years later Laurana was appointed architect of the ducal palace, although Vasari does not name him in his publication, *Lives*, instead attributing the work on the palace to Francesco di Giorgio Martini.

Luciano Laurana, Loggia dei Torricini, Ducal Palace, 1460s, Urbino

Luciano Laurana was undoubtedly the author of the external façade with its superimposed loggias, possibly a variation on the Triumphal Arch of Castelnuovo in Naples. These loggias are characterised by coffered barrel-vaulted ceilings supported by pillars and *all'antica* pilasters with exquisite composite capitals.The loggias demarkate the more private rooms in the palace, the Duke's bedchamber and *studiolo* have walls covered with wooden inlays, which are veritable masterpieces of perspectival illusionism.

FRANCESCO DI GIORGIO MARTINI

Francesco di Giorgio Martini was born in 1439 in Sienna, the city in which he received his eclectic training as a painter, sculptor, architect and engineer. Martini was summoned to Urbino in 1476 to take part in the works on the ducal palace, the reconstruction of the Duomo and the building the churches of San Bernardino and Santa Chiara. The enlightened and culturally avant-garde atmosphere at the court of Federico da Montefeltro had a profound influence on Martini, inspiring him to embark on the first version of his *Treaty on Civil and Military Architecture* during the early 1480s while still in Urbino. His theoretical studies on architecture and Antiquity spurred Martini into deep reflection on building typologies and the anthropomorphical aspects of composition, which are the most thought-provoking part of his writings. In his later years, thanks to his technical engineering skills, he was given the opportunity to draw up the plans for the lantern for the Duomo in Milan. Martini had known and spent time with da Vinci in Milan. The two men had a great many interests in common; they travelled to Pavia together for a consultation on the cathedral that was in the process of being built. Martini would undoubtedly have come across the plans for the Duomo in Pavia as well as the Duomo in nearby Certosa which he was sure to have visited while in Lombardy. These churches evidently made such an impression on him that he reinterpreted them in various different versions in the typological case studies in his treaty.

Francesco di Giorgio Martini, Santa Maria delle Grazie al Calcinaio, begun 1485, Cortona, Arezzo

The church close to Cortona has a largely civic value as it was erected by the populace to give thanks to the Virgin Mary for a miraculous event. The plan layout of the church, the shape of a Latin cross, is greatly simplified and is characterised by a broad single nave flanked by semicircular chapels built into the perimeter walls and which culminate in the luminous central cupola. The interior, which is abstract and graphic in its chromatic and formal linearity, is articulated by dark fasciae and cornices and measured sculptural architectural order typical of Martini's work.

Piero della Francesca, The Brera
Madonna or *Sacra Conversazione*,
c.1469–1472, Milan, Pinacoteca di
Brera (left) and Francesco di
Giorgio Martini, San Bernardino,
post 1482, Urbino (below)

The church of San Bernardino — on
which building probably began after
the death of Federico da Montefeltro
in 1482 — was commissioned by the
Duke as his personal sepulchral temple. The plan of the church features a
short barrel-vaulted nave, culminating
in a square triapsidal space with a
columns at each corner, in a scheme
directly drawn from ancient mau-
solea. The volumetric structure, with
the perspectival axis accentuated by
the barrel vault that terminates in the
end niche — now regrettably remodelled — seems to have been a recurring motif in works executed for
Federico da Montefeltro. It also features in the tiny Cappella del Perdono
within the ducal palace and, incredi-
bly, also in Piero della Francesca's
Brera Madonna or *Sacra
Conversazione*, which is now in the
Brera in Milan. The painting was originally in the church of San Bernardino
in Urbino and dates from between
1469 and 1472. It shows Duke
Federico da Montefeltro kneeling in a
church that appears to be Martini's
church, given its classical and centralised shapes.

MILITARY ARCHITECTURE

With the introduction of firearms, the reality of war underwent a paradigm shift during the quattrocento, which, in turn had a profound effect on architecture. The high, thin medieval walls gave way to massive polygonal constructions, characterised by low, buttressed walls, required to withstand the violence of the blows. The need for artillery-proof defences led to the development of circular or triangular towers on the corners of the star-shaped complexes that constituted the new Renaissance fortresses. The many drawings of fortifications that illustrate Francesco di Giorgio Martini's treaty are proof of the depth of his studies and remain one of the most credible testaments to 15th century military techniques. Martini's military theories, based on an experimental and practical approach were, however, the product of a typically humanist mentality where anthropomorphical principles regulated the forms of cities and fortresses. Martini's successful approach led to his being commissioned to design the fortresses of Mondavio, San Leo and Sassocorvaro for both Federico da Montefeltro and his brother-in-law, Giovanni della Rovere.

Martini's fortified constructions were not constructed in the weaker parts of the territory, as was usually the case, but were rather erected within villages in order to create a dominant relationship with the urban fabric serving to reflect the Duke's power over his subjects. The concept of the fortress, moreover, dovetailed with Martini's anthropomorphical vision: like the head, it was the intellectual guide and ultimate anthropological limit of the human body.

opposite page
Francesco di Giorgio Martini, view and plans for the Rocca di Sassocorvaro, 1470–80s, Urbino

The fortress at Sassocorvaro — unanimously attributed to Francesco di Giorgio — was built for Count Ottaviano Ubaldini, at the periphery of the town, cutting off its access. The plan of the fortress, which consists of towers and fortified walls that curve widely around an internal courtyard, creates an overall shape rather like that of a tortoise shell.

Francesco di Giorgio Martini, Rocca di Mondavio, 1490s, Urbino

The fortress is documented as being designed by Francesco di Giorgio; it was executed for Giovanni della Rovere at Mondavio. The Rocca is undeniably one of his better-preserved fortresses. The complex consists of various buildings, which are encircled by a moat, with a massive octagonal keep that also includes the residential quarters.

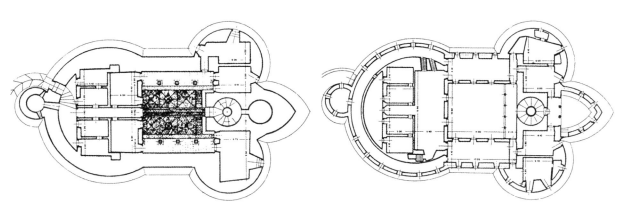

FLORENCE UNDER LORENZO IL MAGNIFICO

During the 1480s Florence reached the pinnacle of its financial prosperity, becoming the focus of an urban remodelling and updating project driven by Lorenzo de' Medici, which involved all the city's leading architects. Medici's aim was to transform the urban face of Florence, as underscored by a ruling in 1489, which provided for the abolition of tax on new buildings, according to a plan to deal with the significant increase in the population. There are various suggestions that Lorenzo, himself, dabbled in architecture, keeping abreast of projects for other patrons and owning his own personal copy of Vitruvius's *De Architectura*.

Brunelleschi's death in 1446 signalled a change in Florentine architecture, with greater use of sculptural decoration and a decidedly more powerful trend to *all'antica* features. This can be ascribed to the greater role of sculptors and carpenters in architectural works as well as to the passion of the wealthy patrons for the precious objects, medals, bronzes and bas reliefs that circulated the courts, helping to ignite a taste for archaeological pieces. Giuliano da Sangallo, the Giuliano brothers, Benedetto da Maiano and Baccio Pontelli were toiling in the city's workshops on pieces where the classical fin de siècle vocabulary was being adapted to the models formalised a few decades earlier by Brunelleschi and Alberti. Giuliano da Sangallo quickly became Lorenzo il Magnifico's favoured architect, producing several different designs for the façade of San Lorenzo and building the Villa at Poggio a Caiano, Lorenzo's private residence in the Florentine countryside.

opposite page
Benedetto da Maiano and Simone del Pollaiolo known as il Cronaca, Palazzo Strozzi, begun 1489, Florence

Filippo Strozzi is known to have consulted Lorenzo il Magnifico about the proportions for this palazzo, which was built in the city centre in an urban block occupied by the Strozzi family. The prototype for the building was the Palazzo Medici, where Michelozzo had remodelled a floor plan drawn from Vitruvius, with the tripartition of the storeys and the mullioned windows. The exterior façades of the palazzo, each side of which is detached, is completely rusticated with hammered blocks of ashlar that become progressively thinner the higher up they ascend.

Giuliano da Sangallo, Sacristy vestibule, Santo Spirito, 1488–1489, Florence

The sacristy in Santo Spirito is evidence of Giuliano da Sangallo's embrace of the trend towards architectural ornamentation and 'antiquing' during the age of Lorenzo il Magnifico.

The coffered barrel vault in the small aperture, supported by pillars, features a carved archaeological scheme drawn from Roman models. Sangallo was, in fact, well acquainted with Roman antiquities, having made painstaking and precise surveys of them during his sojourn in Rome during 1465.

THE MASTERPIECE
THE VILLA AT POGGIO A CAIANO

The Medici family's penchant for rural residences started with Cosimo the Elder, who planned several interventions to the Villa di Cafaggiolo and the Villa del Trebbio in the Mugello area. Both were medieval buildings; impenetrable and fortified and characterised by typical feudal architectural detail. The later residence at Careggi, built in the mid 15th century — where the Accademia Platonica met in 1462 — is proof of a gradual evolution towards a more modern concept of the villa. The same is true of the residence at Fiesole, built by Michelozzo between 1451 and 1457, with its courtyards, loggias and gardens, all elements that serve to relate the dwelling to the contemplative nature of rural indolence. Alberti emphasised the importance of a relationship between a building and its natural surroundings in his treaty, *De Re Aedificatoria*. This con-

cept is illustrated by the front elevation of the Palazzo Piccolomini in Pienza which is orientated towards the valley.

Alberti believed that a building sited on a hillside would be assured of a healthy atmosphere and a visual embrace of the landscape, in an evocative echo of those places held dear in ancient mythology, such as the Parnassus. The palazzo was built by Rosselino in 1459 to a plan most likely designed by Alberti.

Lorenzo de' Medici acquired the land at Poggio a Caiano in 1479 and commissioned his most trusted architect, Giuliano da Sangallo, to design a monumental villa there. The design was to be based on the models and ornamental vocabulary of ancient architecture, which was in turn to become an example for architects pondering the theme of rural residences.

Medici Villa, begun 1485, Poggio a Caiano, Prato

The villa is unusual for its time as it reinterprets the elements of an ancient villa. The archaeological quality is conveyed through the use of an ancient vocabulary that communicates a series of classical elements: the plinth from which the quadrangular volume of the building rises — reminiscent of a *cryptoporticus* — and the loggia shaped like a temple pronaos, crowned by a gable decorated with glazed reliefs depicting the unfolding glories of rural life through the different seasons. The staircase, originally consisting of two rectilinear flights, emphasises the perfect symmetry of the façade and is a forerunner of the dramatic perspectival solutions adopted during the cinquecento era.

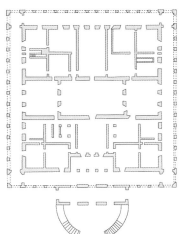

Detail of the loggia vault and plan of the Medici Villa, Poggio a Caiano, Prato

The strictly axial symmetry of the plan is based on the scheme for the residence of the Ancients, as described by Vitruvius. Two sets of rooms adjoin the large barrel-vaulted *sala (hall)*, where decorative detail seems to be a recurrent theme of Giuliano dal Sangallo's, as it is repeated in the vestibule of the sacristy in Santo Spirito as well as the loggia on the façade of the villa, which is decorated with polychrome stucco coffers.

ARCHITECTURAL RENEWAL IN VENICE

Despite the lengthy period of political and economic stability that Venice enjoyed, the city was nevertheless staunchly resilient to the introduction of the classical vocabulary. The reasons for this lay in the city's unique figurative, geographic and architectural tradition, having been subjected for centuries to Byzantine, Arab and Gothic influences. The fact that Venice is built on an island also meant that any architectural renovation was constricted to the predefined urban fabric, deeply influenced by the vagaries of the lagoon and incapable of expansion.

During the quattrocento, the formal configuration of buildings adopted a compromised solution: a mix of partly Gothic and partly Renaissance styles. It was not until the Lombardo brothers and Mauro Codussi went to Venice in 1468, that any serious attempt was made at renovation based on Alberti's architectural schemes. Alberti is known to have been in Venice in 1437. Venice was part of a geographical area that included Padua, Mantua and Ferrara, where cultural exchange led to an updated architectural vocabulary and a trend towards the classical.

The characteristic coloured and chiaroscuro Venetian façades also represented a deep-rooted unique quality which — despite the appearance of new prototypes — continued to define the façades of the city's buildings throughout the Renaissance in a series of sombre spaces and sculptural constructions known only to Venice.

Mauro Codussi, San Michele in Isola, 1469–1478, Venice

The church was built on the island of San Michele di Murano, where the city cemetery is also situated. The church is a sombre and deliberately classical building, far removed from the typical decorative architecture of most Venetian buildings. The vertically tripartite façade is crowned with a semi-circular entablature of Balkan and Dalmatian derivation, and is a modern interpretation of traditional Venetian motifs, some of which had already been employed by Alberti in the original design for the Tempio Malatestiano, undoubtedly a prototype for Codussi's building.

Matteo Raverti and Giovanni Bon, Ca' d'Oro, begun 1423, Venice (left) and Mauro Codussi, Palazzo Vendramin Calergi, c. 1500, Venice (right)

The characteristics of Venetian palaces continued to be passed down from generation to generation over time despite the formal renewal that overtook construction from Mauro Codussi's time onwards.

On either side of the entrance atrium there are spaces equipped for storage and there are two upper stories containing the living spaces. Given the practical impossibility of creating a central courtyard, as exist in Florentine residences, a large *salone (living space)* was built on the first floor, which was lit by high windows overlooking the canal.

The concentration of apertures corresponding to the *sala* on the median axis of the façade gives an indication of the internal layout of the building and defines the horizontal rhythm of the architecture. The Gothic style of the Ca' d'Oro is a reference to the nearby ducal palace, which was re-employed by Codussi for Palazzo Vendramin Calergi, where the traditional features of Venetian palaces are rationalised by the classical language of the orders.

BRAMANTE IN LOMBARDY

Donato Bramante was born in 1444 at Fermignano, near Urbino. According to Vasari Bramante trained as a painter in the workshops of Fra' Carnevale and Piero della Francesca, at the court of Federico da Montefeltro. The mathematical and artistic culture in Urbino as well as Alberti's architectural theories had a profound effect on Bramante and were to become the theoretical rock on which his lengthy and successful career was founded.

Bramante spent time in Lombardy and was at the Sforza court in Milan from 1481 onwards. His first architectural commission was the church of Santa Maria adjacent to San Satiro, embedded in the dense urban fabric, where he was able to employ his gifts as a perspective painter, executing an trompe l'œil bas relief in the choir area to simulate the centrality and symmetry of the layout. Ludovico Sforza dominated Milanese society from the late 1480s onwards. The nobleman was determined to change the face of the city with his new classical vocabulary. He virtually ruled over Milan from 1489 until the turn of the century, involving Bramante in his ambitious renovation programme. Although Bramante came up against the obstinacy of the local masters — seen against the backdrop of traditional building practice and the decorative code of lombard architecture — Milanese figurative culture underwent a transformation spurred on by the presence of da Vinci and 'briefly' Francesco di Giorgio, who helped to promote an updated vocabulary and fuel stimulating debate. Bramante's views, and those of his circle, on three-dimensional space and centralised plan layouts, first formulated in Milan, were to prove fundamental to the evolution of architecture in early 16th century Rome.

opposite page
External view of the apse of Santa Maria delle Grazie, 1492, Milan

The Dominican church of Santa Maria delle Grazie — built by Guiniforte Solari in the 1460s — was part of Ludovico il Moro's remodelling and stylistic updating urban plan for the city of Milan. The reconstruction work, which involved the tribune alone, began in 1492 and focused on creating a large square opening, covered by a cupola according to a plan format that had already been utilised in the Portinari Chapel and the Old Sacristy. The general structured plan of the colossal tribune is evocative of some of the Urbino designs and appears to refer to a design by Bramante, although he cannot be held responsible for the weak and superficial terracotta decoration on the exterior of the building, with its abstract squares and candelabra in an aesthetic typical of traditional Lombardy.

Ruined temple, engraving by B. Prevedari from a drawing by Bramante, 1481, Milan, Civica Raccolta delle Stampe Achille Bertarelli

Only two copies of the engraving exist, which was printed by Bernardino Prevedari and was commissioned by the painter, Matteo Fedeli. The engravings are the first concrete proof of Bramante's presence in Milan. The image depicts a ruined temple; its architectural and formal characteristics are an indication of the directions Bramante and his circle were taking in Milan during that period. It illustrates a centrally planned Greek cross-temple structured in spaces framed by architectural orders, embellished with *all'antica* shell-shaped niches, classical busts and bas relief friezes so typical of northern Italian aesthetic at that time.

opposite page
Donato Bramante and Agostino de Fondulis, Sacristy of Santa Maria presso San Satiro, c. 1483, Milan

The small octagonal, extremely high opening was created by Bramante on the side of the church of San Satiro in an aperture between the building and the surrounding houses. The octagonal plan, with alternating semi-circular and recti-linear niches, follows the well-known scheme for the Milanese Chapel of Sant'Aquilino — as does the typically Lombard motif of the arcaded gallery below the vault.

The medieval building was rebuilt in a completely new style, in a classical vocabulary that brought the articulation of the architectural orders together with a profusion of archaeologically-inspired decorations, featuring candelabra and terracotta busts modelled by Agostino de Fondulis.

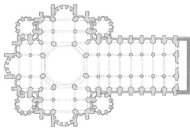

Plan of the original model and view from the Presbytery of the Duomo in Pavia, 1488

The Duomo in Pavia contains more modern architectural elements, remodelled in ancient architectural vocabulary as well as traditional Lombardy schemes.

The plan layout of the church — with its three aisles, semi-circular chapels and centralised cupola-covered presbytery — is drawn from Brunelleschi's plan for Santo Spirito. However, in this case, the central intersecting space has been altered to include piers that transform the polygonal impost of the cupola into an octagon. The addition of a support is a radical alteration to the presbytery, rendering it extremely elongated and giving it a new sculptural monumentality.

The three-dimensional nature of the space can only be ascribed to Bramante; it was a forerunner of his studies for St Peter's Basilica in Rome.

THE MASTERPIECE
THE DUCAL PALACE IN VIGEVANO

Work on Ludovico il Moro's ducal palace in Vigevano, where the Duke kept his rural hunting lodge, took merely two years to complete between 1492 and 1494. The scheme involved turning the public space adjacent to the ancient castle — traditionally used as a market place — into a huge, spectacular forum surrounded by regulated porticoes. The façades were painted with *all'antica* motifs that imbued further grandeur to the House of Sforza. The building of a large square that relegated the to-date communal space into an antechamber to the ducal palace, was the ultimate acknowledgment of the power of Ludovico, who became Duke in 1494. The palace was the jewel in the crown of his fervent propaganda campaign for a return to the imperial glories of Ancient Rome. The ambitious project in which Bramante was involved during the planning stage at least, clearly shows a philological desire to recreate the ancient forum of the Ancients, as Vitruvius described it, later referred to by Alberti in his *De Re Aedificatoria*. The Latin lapidary inscription that Ludovico commissioned for the entrance tower of the castle is confirmation of this, making explicit mention of a *forum* rather than a *platea*.

**View of the Ducal Palace,
1492–1494, Vigevano, Pavia**

LEONARDO DA VINCI IN MILAN

At the request of Lorenzo il Magnifico, Leonardo da Vinci travelled to Milan in 1482 to present his military engineering credentials to the Sforza court. The many and varied interests that made da Vinci the ultimate universal genius meant that he took on a great variety of commissions in Milan, ranging from painting and sculpture, to architecture and civil and military engineering. Da Vinci had no knowledge of Latin, but his profound intelligence and deep curiosity inspired him to study philosophy and literature. He became acquainted with Vitruvius's treaty through the work of Alberti and di Giorgio.

Da Vinci met Bramante in Milan where the two became well acquainted. Da Vinci was also involved in architectural debate over the fundamental issues of that era, this included typological research into centralised plans as well as urban planning theory. Despite his reputation as an architect as mentioned by both Pacioli and Vasari, there are no actual works attributed solely to him, although he was consulted about the cathedrals in both Milan and Pavia. However, the vast number of sketches of churches, palaces and city maps that embellish his manuscripts, bear witness to his deep-rooted interest in architecture. Most of his theoretical work belongs to his Milanese period and largely consisted of architectural research and planning at the Sforza court. Of his manuscripts — collected by Francesco Melzi and later taken apart and reassembled by the sculptor, Pompeo Leoni — that entered the Biblioteca Ambrosiana in the 18th century, only the Atlantic Codex, which was returned to Italy after the fall of Napoleon, remains in Milan.

Leonardo da Vinci, drawing of a central plan church, Paris, Bibliothèque de l'Institut de France, MsB vol. 91v and 22r

Da Vinci's codices contained a great many drawings of centrally planned churches, most of them dating back to his Milanese period. His studies of antique and modern structures — frequently annotated and described — informed his formulation of highly structured plans, containing a central polygonal space covered with a cupola along with smaller *celle* which resulted in further volumes being generated. The various and increasingly complicated variations appear to find a recurring theme in the Greek cross inscribed in a square, with a larger central cupola accompanied by four smaller ones (quincunx). The geometric juxtaposition of volumes diminishing in height from the centre outwards and the monumental plastic wall structure preceded Bramante's research into the quincunx of St Peter's by just a few years.

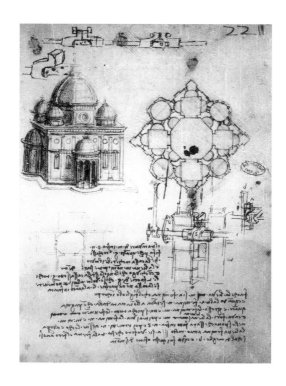

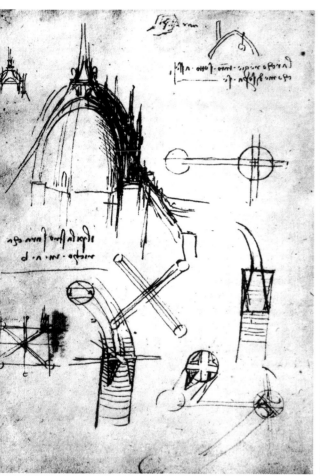
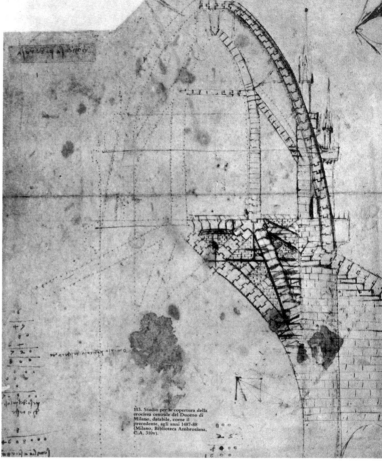

Leonardo da Vinci, sketches for the *tiburio* in the Duomo in Milan, Milan, Biblioteca Trivulziana, Codex Trivulziano, 22v and Milan, Biblioteca Ambrosiana, Codex Atlantico 310rb

After the death of Guiniforte Solari in 1481, the search for a stable and an aesthetically pleasing roof structure for the great intersection crossing remained unresolved — triggering a twenty-year series of consultations and designs. Da Vinci was involved for the first time in 1487 and later, in 1490 when he took part in a consultation along with Bramante and Francesco di Giorgio. Da Vinci's many drawings illustrate that the major problem lay with the challenge of the structural engineering. The dome required a bracing system to deal with the huge loads. From a formal point of view, da Vinci's solution of a cupola connected to the *extrados* and surrounded by pinnacles was a classical one. His design was rejected in July 1490 in favour of one by the Lombard sculptor, Giovanni Antonio Amadeo.

THE EARLY CINQUECENTO

At the turn of the 16th century, Rome was fast over-taking Florence as the main hub of intellectual and architectural endeavour. The building model formulated by Leon Battista Alberti was being adapted to suit the various requirements of the leading Roman prelates and ecclesiasts. One of the first examples of this was the renovation of the Palazzo della Cancelleria, thought to have been initiated by the architect, Baccio Pontelli for Cardinal Raffaele Riario. This was a building where the complexity of the plan was concealed behind a system of pilasters adorning the exterior in a clear, monumental language that masks the inner complexity of the building form.

The plan of the palace made sense of the so-called *piano nobile,* or the first floor, which accommodated the principal reception rooms and was an immediate success due, in part, to the newly changed social and financial status of its patrons.

Antonio da Sangallo the Younger,
Courtyard of Palazzo Baldassini,
1514–1517, Rome

**Palazzo della Cancelleria,
c. 1490, Rome**

The vast residence of Cardinal
Raffaele Riario, powerful head of the
Apostolic Chancery, was undoubtedly
the most important 15th century villa
in Rome. The villa was built in 1490,
although the identity of the architect
who designed it remains an enigma; it
may, in fact, have been the work of
several architects, including, perhaps
Baccio Pontelli. The architectural elements articulating the exterior of the
building were a modern interpretation
of antique models and were a reference to the work of his contemporaries, Alberti and Bramante. It also
echoed Laurana's courtyard for
Federico di Montefeltro in Urbino. The
rhythm of the pilasters framing the
windows on the two upper storeys
determines a rhythmic succession
clearly influenced by Bramante and
which suggests his potential involvement in the design. However,
Bramante did not arrive in Rome
until later in 1500.

**opposite page
Fra' Giocondo, reconstruction of an
ancient house, from Vitruvius,
De Architectura, 1511, vol. 65r
(right) and Antonio di Pellegrino for
Bramante, design for Palazzo dei
Tribunali, Florence, Gabinetto
Disegni and Stampe degli Uffizi,
136A (left)**

The ancient house, as described by
Vitruvius and graphically reconstructed by Fra'Giocondo in his 1511
edition of *De Architectura* established
the basic residential prototype for the
entire quattrocento and cinquecento
period. The layout is based on an axial
symmetry; it has an entrance
vestibule with various rooms grouped
around a porticoed courtyard, the
ancient *peristylium*, which leads to
the private chapel.
This scheme, first reworked in 1444
by Michelozzo di Bartolomeo for the
Palazzo Medici in Florence, was highly
acclaimed during the High Renaissance
in Rome and was reproduced by
Bramante in his 1508 design for the
great Palazzo dei Tribunali in Via
Giulia, which remained surprisingly
true to Fra' Giocondo's original
drawing.

Palazzo Caprini, designed by Bramante sometime after 1501, marked the definitive aesthetic and functional division of building parts: the façade features a high rusticated plinth on the ground level with sculptural double Doric columns on the *piano nobile*, corresponding closely to the appearance of a dwelling *all'antica*. Unlike any building up to that time, Bramante gave a technically revolutionary twist to the classical vocabulary, eschewing the use of stone in favour of less expensive materials, such as bricks, which he finished with plaster in order to make them look like travertine. This enabled those less well-off the chance to build presigious residences of their own without necessitating too much capital investment. Equally, the fact that the middle classes were becoming more affluent meant that there was greater demand for grand dwellings that did not necessarily require the investment of large amounts of money: the quasi sculptural *romanitas* of the elevation combined with economic construction costs meant that buildings of this sort became established as a new building typology that was to be frequently emulated over the coming years and would enjoy enormous success in northern Italy with Raphael and Giulio Romano, Sansovino and Palladio.

Numerous dwellings, which adhered to the composition of large palaces with a vestibule, a courtyard and private apartments, though on a smaller scale,

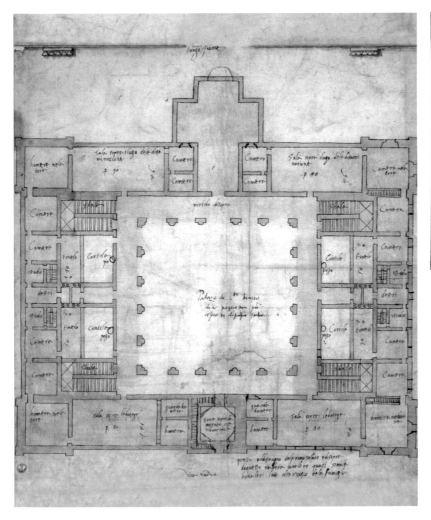

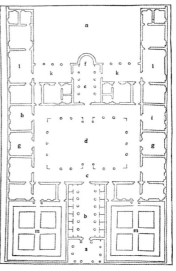

thus sprang up in Rome during this period. Palazzo Baldassini (Antonio da Sangallo, 1513), Palazzo Branconio dell'Aquila (Raphael, 1519) and Palazzo Massimo alle Colonne (Peruzzi, 1532) all fall into this category. While these smaller palaces were being built for less renowned clients, Antonio da Sangallo the Younger started work in 1513 on the monumental Palazzo Farnese for Cardinal Alessandro, the future Pope Paul III. The palazzo, with its sober façade, devoid of orders, echoes the composition of Florence's Palazzo Medici and Palazzo Strozzi and its simple exterior became the primary model for Roman palaces during the late cinquecento.

The golden age of the imperial villa

The typological and formal renewal to which the urban residences of the nobility and rich bourgeoisie were subjected also extended to their rural residences, places of leisure and recreation that emulated the suburban dwellings of bygone eras.

During the early cinquecento in Rome buildings designed according to the enclosed, still somewhat fortified structure of Villa Medici at Poggio a Caiano gave way to more open schemes with loggias and terracing. These villas paved the way for the gardens *all'italiana* that were to become an integral part of country residences.

Bramante's grandiose courtyard for the Belvedere, intended to resemble a huge theatre in which spectacular shows could be held, was the focalpoint of Pope Julius II's renovation scheme for the Vatican Palace. Bramante designed an enormous open area, over three hundred metres in length for the Pope, spectacularly terraced and culminating in a large *exedra*, along the architectural lines of the imperial palaces of Julius Cesaer and the Temple of Fortuna at Palestrina — a frequently recurring icon for monumental buildings of the Renaissance.

Marteen van Hemskerk, The terrace at Villa Madama, 1530s, Berlin, Staatliche Museen zu Berlin, Kupferstichkabinett, Berliner Skizzenbücher, 79D2 24r

Marteen van Hemskerk's impression of the terrace at Villa Madama, which he drew during his Italian sojourn, illustrates clearly the strict adherence of early 16th century Roman designs to the dictates of ancient architecture. The villa was partly built by Raphael and his circle of architects; it reformulated the splendour of imperial villas with its profusion of decorative elements which drew directly from classical ruins. The ideal fusion of nature and architecture in Raphael's design achieves a classical and monumental harmony and was to pave the way for the mounting vogue for architectonic gardens.

From 1506, da Vinci focused on tackling the question of bringing architecture and nature together in his design for the residence of Charles d'Amboise that was never realised. Surviving sketches show a large villa with a loggia opening onto a garden containing minutely detailed water features and numerous species of birds and flowers.

The renaissance of the imperial villa in its complete form is exemplified by Raphael's design for Villa Madama, on the slopes of Monte Mario, which was commissioned by Pope Leo X. It is an ambitious reworking of the Renaissance elements; the grandeur and functionality of the ancient residences. Villa Madama boasts loggias, fishponds and hanging gardens, as well as a theatre, a hippodrome and thermal baths.

During Leo X's papacy, between 1513 and 1521, the formal adherence to ancient classic models was at its zenith. This era was driven by the synergy created by the desire for presige on one hand and on the other, the wealth of financial opportunities open to patrons of culture who aspired to bask in the glory of the Golden Age in Rome.

Baldassarre Peruzzi, Palazzo Massimo alle Colonne, begun 1532, Rome

Baldassarre Peruzzi inverted the structural order defined by Bramante's Palazzo Caprini in his façade for Palazzo Massimo, which has a vestibule screened by columns on the ground floor. The columns extend along the closed side wings of the building, where they provide structural support for the three upper floors. The curvature of the façade, the central part of which is convex, is aligned with the entrance on Via del Paradiso. The curve is likely to have been dictated, not just by the foundations of an ancient stadium, but also by the shape of the Teatro di Marcello, characterised by a series of structures adjoined to the outer wall.

BRAMANTE IN ROME

The dawn of the new century saw the geographical transfer of architectural debate from north central Italy southwards to Rome. Milan was conquered by the French in 1499, prompting Bramante, who was already one of the most highly regarded architects of the period, to leave Lombardy for Rome, where within a few short years he became a major figure. Pope Julius II, born Giuliano della Rovere, was elected in October 1503. A powerful and determined patron of the arts, Julius II invested a substantial amount of money in the renovation of some of the most significant pontifical buildings, such as the Vatican Palace and St Peter's Basilica, as part of an ambitious programme intended to glorify the papacy and the Roman Catholic Church. The papal coffers were kept from emptying thanks to the Pope's alliance with Agostino Chigi, the wealthiest and most powerful banker of the period, who was both a friend and a relative by marriage. The projects commissioned by the Pope were driven by his enormous personal ambition. Julius II saw the renaissance of classical antiquity as the ideal, grandiose and triumphal means of transforming Rome from a medieval city into the heart of the empire, with himself as the new 'Julius Caesar'. The consequence of the new scale urban planning requirements and the financial strength of the Roman scheme, compared with the earlier examples in the cities of Urbino and Milan, was a leap in scale that also pertained to the new architecture, which was modelled on the grandiose, monumental, imperial works of Ancient Rome, such as the gigantic thermal baths, the Domus Aurea and Villa Adriana. Julius's death, in 1513, preceeded that of Bramante by only one year, but the *renovatio imperii* dream was nevertheless carried forward by Pope Leo X.

Donato Bramante, Cloister of Santa Maria della Pace, 1500–1504, Rome

The cloister of the convent of Lateran canons was commissioned in 1500 by the protector of the monks, Cardinal Oliviero Carafa. Bramante created a perfectly symmetrical and biaxial space, its proportions dictated by a modular grid that determined its dimensions. Bramante's study of extant orders led him to adopt the *all'antica* classical approach and to avoid using columns as supports for the arches, rather building sixteen square piers. On the upper level, Corinthian piers aligned to those on the ground floor are crowned with an architrave; they alternate between slender columns scaled according to the size of the supports. In order to adhere to the basic grid, Bramante reduced the size of the Ionic pilasters in the corners, enabling the piers to become composite.

**Donato Bramante, Spiral staircase in the Belvedere courtyard,
1503–1504, Vatican City**

Bramante built the magnificent spiral staircase on the east side of the Belvedere to provide a link from the great courtyard to the lower-level Viale Angelico and Via Trionfale and also to be able to transport building materials down to the courtyard.

The curved staircase consists of four ramps, each with eight columns articulated in Tuscan, Doric, Ionic and Corinthian orders respectively according to the rules of canonical succession drawn from ancient models. The columns on the ramp support a simplified entablature consisting of a slender architrave and an elongated frieze, which rises to the ceiling. The column shafts grow more slender as they rise; thus the 1:5 ratio of the first Tuscan column has been reduced to 1:8.4 in the final Corinthian column. This extraordinary device, without precedent in Bramante's earlier work, is testament to his incredible versatility and his ability to work with equal confidence on an urban scale as on minute detail. This scheme also indicates Bramante's ability to discard existing models in favour of a compositional freedom that is thoroughly innovative and modern.

THE MASTERPIECE
SAN PIETRO IN MONTORIO, ROME

The complex architectural and symbolic programme that inspired the design of the *tempietto* of San Pietro in Montorio should be examined with the knowledge of Bramante's fervent studies on Roman antiquities. Bramante's creativity, underpinned by his profound ability to synthesise his knowledge and his extensive humanist approach, found its expression in the creation of philologically classical architecture such as the Belvedere courtyard and the *tempietto* of San Pietro in Montorio, which both Serlio and Palladio believed deserved to be seen on a par with the 'immortal' works of Antiquity.

The *tempietto,* designed in 1503–1505, is a small but significant structure; it was commissioned by Bernardo De Carvajal, a Cardinal at the Holy Cross in Jerusalem and Procurator of the King of Spain, in honour of the martyrdom of St Peter at the spot where his crucifixion was believed to have taken place. The original concept, which was never realised but was discussed by Serlio in his treaty, seems to have been to erect the *tempietto* in the centre of a circular arcaded courtyard adjacent to the church of San Pietro al Gianicolo, which had been consecrated in 1500. The layout of Bramante's *sacellum* was a reworking of the peripteral temple described by Vitruvius and was influenced by illustrious ancient buildings, such as the Temple of Vesta in Rome and the Tivoli temple. The perfection and harmony of the circular shape, representative of the world and the cosmic universe, was also a powerful trigger of humanist thought from the time of Alberti onwards and portrayed a powerful image of the first Pope and founder of the Roman Catholic Church.

opposite page
Donato Bramante, *Tempietto* at San Pietro in Montorio, c. 1503–1505, Rome

The plan of the *tempietto* is characterised by the volumetric superimposition of three aspects: the underground crypt (representing the underworld), the *cella* with the peripteral circle of columns (representing the earthly dimension and St Peter's controversial church) and finally the cupola, (representing the triumphant Church of Christ).
From an architectural perspective the *tempietto* was the fruit of Bramante's reflections on the trilithic system previously employed in the cloister of the church of Santa Maria della Pace. Here, the columns resume their load-bearing function and support a continuous entablature crowned with a baluster, while the internal walls of the *cella* are articulated by pilasters that regulate the wall mass.

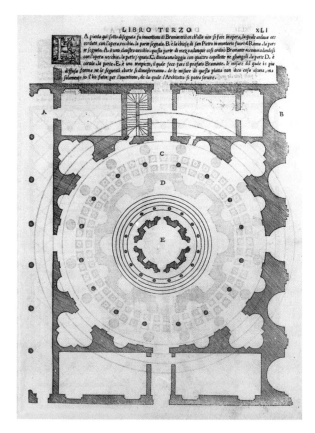

Sebastiano Serlio, Plan for the *Tempietto* at San Pietro in Montorio within a circular courtyard, Sette libri dell'architettura, Book Three, Venice, 1540, vol. 41

The design that Sebastiano Serlio reproduced conforms to Bramante's original concept of building a circular courtyard around the *tempietto*. Its circularity and symmetry are emphasised by the device of the circle inscribed in a square, which recalls Vitruvius's *homo ad circulum* humanist symbol. The axes of symmetry identify four orthogonal points and four diagonal lines which — with the eight niches, two per side — and sixteen columns, appear to define a symbolic plan based on Vitruvius's mathematical speculations and the Christian sanctity of the number eight, which is linked to the Passion and resurrection of Christ.

THE FOUNDATION OF THE NEW BASILICA OF ST PETER'S

The ancient basilica erected by Emperor Constantine on the site of St Peter's grave, alongside the Vatican Palace, played a major part in Pope Julius's ambitious renovation programme. Pope Nicholas V and Bernardo Rossellino, his architect, had previously embarked on a plan to renovate the medieval façade of the church and had already made alterations to the eastern end of the building by inserting a choir and a cupola. Pope Julius, however, sought to completely rebuild the basilica to a modern and grandiose design in order, in part, to celebrate his own earthly glory by placing his sepulchral monument — commissioned to Michelangelo — in the choir. Bramante's earliest designs probably date from around 1505 after he had successfuly presented his plans for the Belvedere to Pope Nicholas. Bramante's plan, an enormous Greek cross inscribed in a square, according to his conception of the central plan, was replaced the following year by a new design, in which the choir was built according to Rossellini's foundations and a short nave led up to the central intersection.

In the final design, Peter's tomb, situated under the altar in the centre of the tribune, preceded Pope Julius's chapel, which was in the rear choir, richly decorated with mosaics and lit by seven large windows. The construction works, which had advanced as far as the impost of the cupola, were interrupted by Pope Julius's death in 1513, followed by Bramante's death shortly thereafter in 1514. Subsequent alterations to the design by Raphael, Sangallo and Peruzzi were only to achieve a new synthesis with Michelangelo under the papacy of Pope Paul III years later.

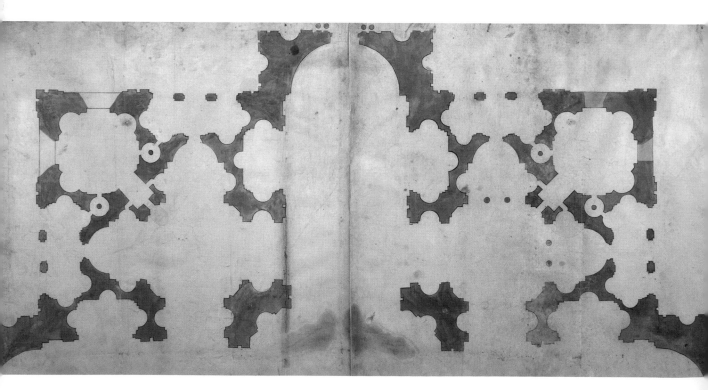

opposite page
Donato Bramante, Plan drawn on parchment for the St Peter's Basilica, 1505, Florence, Gabinetto Disegni and Stampe degli Uffizi, 1A

The 'parchment plan' was Bramante's first design for the renovated St Peter's Basilica and also appears to represent Pope Julius II's ideal plan. The Pope had the plan engraved on the foundation medal made by Caradosso in 1505. The scheme, a Greek cross inscribed in a square, was the culmination of Bramante's reflections on multicentric centralised plans in which a higher central body covered with a cupola branches out into smaller, subsidiary spaces. The quincunx plan, which is Byzantine in origin and was reworked several times in sketches by da Vinci, who had spent several years in Milan at the same time as Bramante, represents the idea of Celestial Jerusalem, confident, enclosed by walls and configured as the ideal shape of the universe, in which the earth, at the centre, extends to all four corners of the universe.

Marteen van Hemskerk, View of St Peter's Basilica under construction, Berlin, Staatliche Museen zu Berlin, Kupferstichkabinett, Berliner Skizzenbücher, vol. 13 r

Marteen van Hemskerk's perspective drawings provide the most trustworthy impressions of the state of the building works prior to their resumption under Pope Paul III. The drawings show the great central opening of the basilica, built to the design of 1506. The four enormous piers, which form the support structure for the cupola and formed one of the most innovative elements of Bramante's construction, are to be clearly seen.
The wedge-shaped form of the piers meant that they acted not only as buttresses for the enormous load from the dome, but also maximised the amount of space for the presbytery. The implementation of the concept of the round-cornered square, which articulates the overall plan, set an architectural trend that lasted until the Neoclassical era.

ARCHITECTURE OF RAPHAEL, PERUZZI AND WORKS COMMISSIONED BY AGOSTINO CHIGI

Bramante was regarded by his contemporaries — after Brunelleschi — as the new master of architecture, his work made a deep impression on his peers and soon becoming the primary point of reference for the study of design. The artist, Raphael, was born in Urbino, the cradle of humanist perspective and painted *The School of Athens* in the Stanza della Segnatura in the Vatican in 1508. The architectural background of the fresco was modelled on the great, majestic central space in St Peter's Basilica. The exponents of the *maniera moderna* conditioned by their own experiences and places of origin, reworked Bramante's œuvre. Rome became an artistic hotbed of stimuli and cultural exchange, a linguistic dialect striving for a common set of rules. The work of Raphael, Sangallo and Peruzzi, along with the many schemes that they drew up for the St Peter's Basilica following Bramante's death are the exceptional outcome of a unique period in history, in which the cultural heritage and experimental curiosity of the artists of that epoch were allowed to flourish thanks to their enlightened and financially secure patrons. The tremendously wealthy Sienese banker, Agostino Chigi, who shared some of the Pope's financial interests and was himself an ambitious patron, played a fundamental role in the history of Renaissance patronage. Chigi commissioned his own funeral mausoleum and magnificent residence in Rome, which were built by two of the most famous architects of the time, his compatriots Baldassarre Peruzzi and Raphael — the two most well-renowned architects of the time.

opposite page
Baldassarre Peruzzi, Sala delle Colonne at Villa Chigi, known as the Farnesina, begun 1505, Rome

Baldassarre Peruzzi, originally from Sienna, moved to Rome in 1503; he was known to have been working on the construction of Agostino Chigi's villa a few years later. It is probable that he finished building the direct predecessor of this villa typology, the Villa alle Volte in Sienna, which had been designed a few years earlier, in 1505, by Francesco di Giorgio for the Chigi family. Inside the Farnesina, situated at the gates of Rome, Peruzzi executed an admirable trompe-l'œil *veduta* of a city framed by exquisitely detailed twin columns.

Raphael, Chigi Chapel at Santa Maria del Popolo, 1511, Rome

The memorial chapel for Agostino Chigi, started in 1511, is an extraordinarily eloquent small classical space, clearly influenced by the exacting proportions of Bramante's *tempietto*. The general layout, however, is a reinterpretation of the tribune in St Peter's Basilica. The monumental, ancient Corinthian order that forms the supports and also frames the great archway of the door echoes the Pantheon.

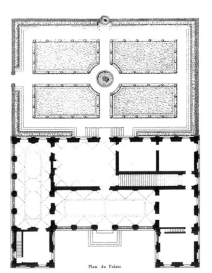

Plan du Palais.

Plan of the Sala delle Colonne at Villa Chigi, known as the Farnesina, by P. M. Letarouilly, Edifices de Rome Moderne, 1868–1874, Paris

Agostino Chigi's residence is characterised by a layout where two wings branch off the central body of the building to frame a porticoed loggia in the centre. The relatively simple geometric scheme contrasts with the villa's sumptuously ornate interior decor.

DWELLINGS ALL'ANTICA: THE ROMAN PALACE

The *all'antica* vocabulary, increasingly classical and antiquarian, was employed during this period not only for the grandiose papal buildings, but also to define the many buildings commissioned by wealthy cardinals and private patrons belonging to the great Roman noble families: Agostino Chigi, Giulio Alberini, Melchiorre Baldassini, Jacopo da Brescia and Giovanbattista Branconio who all had residences built *'all'antica'*, where the classical vocabulary represented the height of modernity and social status. The geometric scheme that reinterpreted the Florentine quadrangular format with rooms grouped around a porticoed courtyard still derived from the reconstruction of Vitruvius's antique houses, while the architecture evolved in a sophisticated classical and true to the Antique. The demand for prestigous residences for

Antonio Lafréry, Palazzo Caprini, Rome, from Speculum Romanae Magnificentiae, Rome 1559–1602 (top) and façade of Palazzo Caprini, London, Royal Institute of British Architects, SC 223/XIV, 11 (below)

Donato Bramante built the villa for Adriano Caprini of Viterbo, a high-ranking member of the Curia, between 1501 and 1510. The villa, which no longer exists, marked a revolutionary approach to designing private residences and became one of the most emulated and studied models of the entire Renaissance, up to and beyond Palladio's time. The rusticated plinth, devoid of orders, with rectangular apertures and lunettes, was surmounted by a first floor with applied Classical orders framing pedimented windows and supporting a classically Vitruvian Doric entablature.

The appearance of the villa, markedly *all'antica*, unlike any other building before it, was achieved with the use of inexpensive materials such as brick, plaster and stucco finished to look like travertine, thus enabling a prestigious, classical dwelling which could be built with limited financial means.

the enlightened new bourgeoisie that were not exhorbitant to build, resulted in the development of the new wave of houses, with space for workshops on the ground floor, which guaranteed a steady income for their proprietor, and genteel apartments on the upper floor. The elongated rectilinear sites of many of the small palaces in Rome — facing onto the street — during this period were offset by the huge, orthogonal bulk of the imposing and monumental Palazzo Farnese, which was freestanding. The construction of the palazzo took many years and many different architects were involved in the building process. The Palazzo Farnese, which was modelled on Palazzo Medici and Palazzo Strozzi in Florence, was greatly popular during the second half of the cinquecento in Rome.

Antonio da Sangallo the Younger, Palazzo Farnese, begun 1514, Rome

The new villa for Cardinal Alessandro Farnese was erected behind Via Giulia, the street created by the Pontiff as a link between the Vatican and Bramante's Palazzo dei Tribunali. Antonio da Sangallo the Younger, who joined his uncle Giuliano in Rome in the early 16th century, designed a freestanding building with a generous internal courtyard. The villa is accessed through a rectangular colonnaded opening three bays wide, modelled on the antique vestibules described by Vitruvius and illustrated in Fra' Giocondo's edition of *De Architectura*. The exterior façade, finished with plaster, is characterised by robustly rusticated edges, an economising device that was to prove extremely popular. When Pope Alexander was elected in 1534, he opened the area in front of the villa to be made into the great Piazza Farnese and, on Sangallo's death in 1454, commissioned Michelangelo to complete the unfinished upper floor of the building.

THE MASTERPIECE
VILLA MADAMA IN ROME

On the death of Pope Julius II in 1513, Lorenzo il Magnifico's son, Giovanni de' Medici, was elected to the papacy, taking the title of Leo X. He was eager to be an equal to his predecessor with regard to the renovation of pontifical buildings.

The idea of a private dwelling, to be built in a prominent position on the north-eastern slopes of Monte Mario with a view of the Tiber and across Rome, dates back to 1516 and is indicative of the Pope's desire to continue the tradition of the sumptuous Medici villas erected by his predecessors on Florentine territory. Work began in earnest in 1518 according to a design by Raphael and was overseen by the Pope's cousin, Giulio Romano, later destined to become Pope Clement VI; the nominal patron of the villa.

A year after building work commenced, Romano also sought the expertise of Antonio da Sangallo the Younger, who seems to have played a purely technical role in the project. This primarily involved the consolidation of the site and his engagement to continue with the project after Raphael's death in 1520 with the help of Romano. The complex was never completed, but is well documented in drawings by Raphael, Sangallo and their colleagues. The complex consisted of an imposing residence overlooking the valley and, according to the plans, was to be articulated by a giant order of pilasters alternating with tripartite *serliana* apertures, thus portraying a grandiose image of the power of the Medici dynasty. The layout of the villa, with its alternating enclosed apartments, loggias and terraces was modelled on imperial buildings and villas described in classical literature, as well as on the Belvedere, designed thirteen years earlier by Bramante. The villa was the direct antecedent and most important point of reference for the residence of Pope Leo X.

opposite page
Raphael, Loggia at Villa Madama, 1518, Rome

Villa Madama's close relationship with the surrounding landscape, previously remodelled by Alberti along the lines of the ancient villa described by Pliny the Younger, was emphasised by the classical and archaeologically-inspired colonnaded loggia, decorated with frescoes of grotesques by Giovanni da Udine, which were a reproduction of those at the Domus Aurea.

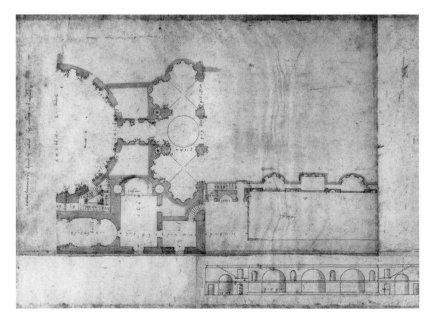

Andrea Palladio, Plan for Villa Madama, London, Royal Institute of British Architects, SC 217/X/18

Andrea Palladio's study, executed between 1541 and 1547, illustrates the completed part of the villa, which still remained as Raphael had originally intended. The plan reveals the complexity and monumentality of the villa. The circular courtyard and loggia with its three openings orientated outwards onto the gardens, along a longitudinal axis, unfolded in a series of apartments and terraces.

CENTRAL-PLAN CHURCHES

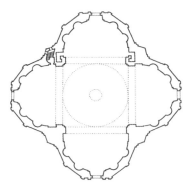

Architectural interest in the centralised composition of religious buildings had been mounting steadily since the early quattrocento. The adherence to the classical language of architecture and the "beautiful manners of ancient buildings" led to renewed interest in Vitruvius's Treaty. In Book Three of the Treaty, which focuses on temples, Vitruvius muses on the proportional perfection of the human figure inscribed in the geometrical shapes of the circle and the square as a generator of geometric schemes. This concept was reworked by Alberti, da Vinci, Filarete and di Giorgio, discussed in every treaty up to the time of Palladio and beyond and remained a fundamental, primary point of reference for all Renaissance architecture. The rigorous geometry of centrally-planned buildings roused the kind of emotions in the artists of the quattrocento and cinquecento that can be traced back to Pythagoras and neoplatonic philosophical theories, which postulate the mathematical harmony of the world and Nature. This theory culminates in Marsilio Ficino's definition of God, Himself, as the centre and circumference of the universe. The reflection on centrally configured churches and their symbolic meaning were illustrated by the numerous antique, or supposedly ancient, buildings in Italy. These projects were analysed, studied and reworked by the architects of that epoch. Centralised church buildings rose to their height during the early cinquecento. This was triggered by the revolutionary synthesis of Bramante's Roman projects and were continued by his many collaborators, who helped to broaden his architectural vocabulary.

View and plan of Santa Maria della Consolazione, begun 1509, Todi, Perugia, late quattrocento/early cinquecento

A large number of centrally planned churches were built in the aftermath of a miraculous event linked to the Virgin Mary, to whom they were then dedicated. These sanctuaries were all civic commissions and were located in isolated places near the city gates, as with this particular church, on which construction started in 1509. The plan of the church, with its simplified and geometric volumes, is characterised by the four tribunes adjacent to a central space surmounted by a cylindrical drum and cupola, which derived from da Vinci's indepth study of multicentric buildings. Archival research has shown that Cola di Matteuccio da Caprarola was in charge of the building works, however it has proved impossible to discover who actually designed the building, which is frequently, yet implausibly, ascribed to Bramante.

Antonio da Sangallo the Elder, View and plan of San Biagio, 1518, Montepulciano, Sienna

San Biago church was built in 1518 for the community of Montepulciano, (possibly also partly due to interest from Cardinale Del Monte, for whom Antonio da Sangallo the Elder had previously conceived the palace at Montepulciano). Sangallo reworked the central plan format, together with a cupola and a bell tower on either side of the façade, reminiscent of the new St Peter's Basilica, which was then still at the construction stage. The structure was based on the Greek cross plan of Santa Maria delle Carceri in Prato, designed many years earlier by his brother Giuliano. The Doric order, which articulates the interior and the base of the exterior, is drawn directly from the Basilica Emilia.

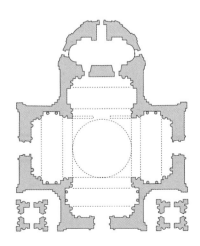

MICHELANGELO IN FLORENCE

Lorenzo il Magnifico's death initiated a lengthy period of political and cultural instability, which also had a destabilising effect on artistic production. Between 1494 and 1498 Florence was under the influence of the religious mysticism espoused by the Dominican friar, Girolamo Savonarola. There was a fervent atmosphere of moral and prophetic renewal that ended with Savonarola's execution at the stake. Gonfaloniere Piero Soderini's republic, which had been in power since 1502, was followed by the return of the Medici family in 1512, who were further empowered by the election of Giovanni de'Medici to the papacy in 1513 when he took the title of Leo X. Despite the triumphal papal celebrations, there were no signs of substantial changes in Florentine architecture. It was not until 1519, when Michelangelo Buonarroti was commissioned to design the New Sacristy at San Lorenzo and the Biblioteca Laurenziana, that there was any significant break with the past and the development of a new Tuscan style. Michelangelo, initially a sculptor and then a painter and architect, was trained in the epoch of the neoplatonic culture of the Medici at San Marco, where he studied ancient sculpture. He then sojourned at length in Rome, where he worked on Pope Julius II's funeral monument as well as on his frescoes in the Sistine Chapel; he did not return to Florence for many years until he was far older. Once back in Florence, Pope Leo X commissioned Michelangelo for his renovation project for the façade of San Lorenzo.

opposite page, top
Michelangelo Buonarroti,
New Sacristy, San Lorenzo,
begun 1519, Florence

Cardinal Giulio, the future Pope Clement VII, commissioned Michelangelo to build the new sacristy at San Lorenzo. The Cardinal had become Governor of Florence on the death of Lorenzo and was keen to have a new sepulchral building constructed for the Medici family. The design was modelled on Brunelleschi's symmetrical Old Sacristy, to a similar square plan covered with a cupola. Michelangelo's sacristy, however, was far more complex, with a high attic below the lunette area rendering the volumetric proportions more slender as they rose. However, the compositional clarity of the Old Sacristy, in which the formal classical interior echoes the articulation of the walls, becomes an ambiguous configuration in the New Sacristy, in which the decorative sculptural elements are not preconditioned by the structure itself.

Michelangelo Buonarroti,
***Ricetto* of the Biblioteca**
Laurenziana, begun 1523, Florence

Building commenced on the library in 1523 after Giulio de' Medici's election to the papacy. The design created three distinct spaces: the *ricetto* (or vestibule), the reading room and an innovative triangular-plan library for rare books which was never realised. The solemn vestibule has a powerfully vertical dynamic, which is accentuated by the formal decoration of the walls. The three superimposed elements of the wall mass are characterised by a deliberate departure from the classical vocabulary and has quirky canonical elements. For instance, the overtly high columns with their Doric capitals and Corinthian bases are built into the wall mass and alternate with blind aedicules with tapering pilasters. The magnificent stairway — for which Michelangelo made numerous designs — was built by Ammannati between 1559–1560. The stair encroaches on the narrow vestibule in a succession of steps that widen in a viscous flow of ovals at floor level.

Michelangelo Buonarroti, Reading room at the Biblioteca Laurenziana, begun 1523, Florence

The graphic, planar simplicity of the room is at odds with the plastic and mannerist *ricetto*. The contrast is heightened by the proportional, volumetric and luminous contrast between the two spaces. The reading room walls are articulated by Doric pilasters which frame windows surmounted by rectangular aedicules in a measured, regular rhythmic sequence. The doors openings in the two small walls are typical examples of Michelangelo's tendency to combine two different formal design solutions. The coffered ceiling, although built later, adhered to Michelangelo's design at the express order of the Pope, who wanted an original decorative scheme that differed from the *all'antica* models so popular in Rome at that time.

MANNERISM AND
THE COUNTER-REFORMATION

The extreme high level of intellectual tension during the early cinquecento in Rome, which coincided with Julius II and part of Leo X's papacy, was not destined to last for a lengthy period. Efforts to match the cultural and civil perfection of ancient Greece and Rome, largely underpinned by on-going study and analysis, appear to have lost momentum by 1520. After Bramante's death, in 1514, his disenchanted disciples found themselves on more solid social and financial ground and became aware of their right to the great humanist cultural heritage. Raphael's clear interpretation of the classical vocabulary of the Vatican gave way, in his final works, to freer experimentation, diverging from the ancient canonical and philological rules. Deviation from the golden rules of the classical language, as defined by Bramante, began to characterise artistic output and was to take divergent courses. This was also due, in part, to the diaspora of artists after the Sack of Rome in 1527. The invasion of the 'Lanzichenecchi' completely devastated the city and marked a profound turning point for art and architecture. Foreign invasion and deep political and religious crisis throughout the Reformation were to ring the final death knell of humanist ideals. Michelangelo, a restless soul by nature, set the trend for a more opulent and dramatic style and a loosening up of the stylistic vocabulary derived from the late cinquecento reliance on textbooks.

Giulio Romano, detail of the frieze at Palazzo Te, begun 1525, Mantua

Pietro Ferrerio, elevation of the façade of Palazzo Branconio dell'Aquila in Rome, *I Palazzi di Roma dei più Celebri Architetti,* **Rome, c. 1655, vol. 40**

The palazzo — of which only a few drawings and an engraving survive — was designed in 1519 by Raphael for Giovanbattista Branconio, *cubicolario* translate to Pope Leo X. The palazzo is regarded as an essential benchmark for the evolution of civil architecture during the first half of the cinquecento.
The classical decoration of the façade, a style that was to become extremely popular during the latter part of the century, is situated above the architectural order and is far removed from the architectural eloquence of Bramante's Palazzo Caprini and the sober simplicity of Palazzo Farnese.

Following the Sack of Rome, programmatic architectural research and design plans began to fall out of favour, along with the ideals that underpinned them. Palazzo Te, designed by Giulio Romano for Federico Gonzaga in 1525, was a signal of the fact that *all'antica* had ceased to be the preferred style of residential renovation, but a more of a whim dependent on courtly ideals and splendour.

The exodus of artists from Rome helped to perpetuate the models previously honed in the capital and opened up new possibilities elsewhere. The palazzo configuration, conceived by Bramante and perfected by his followers, was being continued by Michele Sanmicheli and Jacopo Sansovino in the Veneto. Sanmicheli's Palazzo Canossa of 1526, and his later, Palazzo Bevilacqua, were derived from Vitruvian and 'Bramantesque' models; their classical decoration includes motifs drawn from Roman monuments in Verona.

Residential buildings in Venice were in a league of their own; their proportion was dictated by the particular shape of the aquatic city built on lagoons. By the Middle Ages, the lack of space and light meant that façades were already being built with generous windows on the upper floors, allowing light into the central *salone* and into the residents' living spaces. This occurred even prior to the Renaissance revival of the Vitruvian *vestibulum*, which opened onto the canal. The formal adherence to, and departures from, the Roman model were competently and critically reworked by Sansovino in his projects for Piazza San Marco in 1536 and Palazzo Corner in 1545.

Meanwhile in Rome, Michelangelo was busy designing the buildings enclosing the Piazza del Campidoglio (1539), which echo Bramante's sculptural and imposing plasticity as well as his powerful use of over-scaled orders. Michelangelo was also involved in building Villa Giulia in 1551, according to a design by Vignola for Pope Julius III, in which the spatial themes of Villa Madama were reformulated. The second half of the century saw the emergence of two distinct trends, in Rome and in the Veneto. Sangallo's death, in 1546, was followed by a revival of his work in Rome. In the Veneto, on the

opposite page
Michele Sanmicheli, Palazzo Grimani, 1556–1557, Venice

The façade of the great Palazzo Grimani — to which an upper level was later added that is not attributed to Sanmicheli — looks out over the canal, its large tripartite vestibule can be accessed directly from the water. The tricky alignment of the site made the typical articulation of Venetian buildings, with the windows of the *gran salone* located above the median axis, impossible, forcing Sanmicheli to position the *sala* (hall) off-centre, to the left. The uniformity and monumentality of the façade disguise the fact that the plan is asymmetrical and that the arrangement of the internal spaces is unconventional.

other hand, the different demands of the clientele and the ascent of Andrea Palladio's career led to the creation of new, restrained models.

Palladio's extensive knowledge of ancient architecture led to a personal and innovative interpretation of the ideal Vitruvian house, as early as 1524, with his design of Palazzo Thiene. Palladio was later given the commission to prepare the drawings for his patron, Daniele Barbaro's edition of Vitruvius's texts, published in 1556.

While keeping to the canonical planning format of the *vestibulum*, *atrium* and *peristylium* and axial symmetry of the entrance, Palladio's buildings also allowed him to experiment with various geometric solutions. The evolution of his exterior figurative ornamentation is evidence of his increasing fascination of the ancient Roman models, thus culminating in Palladio's use of half columns surmounted by statues in the manner of triumphal arches. It was in his design of country estates, however, that Palladio truly excelled. The Venetian patrons, who had fled the cities during the second half of the century, found their ideal residences in Palladio's simple, economically constructed, *all'antica* villas. La Rotonda, an isolated and central-plan building modelled on the Roman Pantheon, was the acme of Palladio's attempts to bring together residential and religious architecture. After a century of planning and experimentation, the noble house finally assumed a superior and a representative architectural dignity of its own, despite its 'lowly' function as a mere dwelling place for humans.

Andrea Palladio,
Palazzo Chiericati, 1550, Vicenza

The elongated plan of the palazzo extends into a rectangle, with the entrance opening out from the longer elevation. The façade is articulated by freestanding columns that create a portico at street level as well as two symmetrical loggias on the first floor, which are separated by a slightly protruding central bay. The unconformity of the building derives from Palladio's conscious intention to recreate an *all'antica* forum on the Piazza dell'Isola, which is enclosed by classical colonnades on both floors, as described in ancient texts and by Vitruvius. The configuration of Palazzo Chiericati was unique in Palladio's œuvre; it is a combination of two residential typologies — both city palazzo and villa. The palazzo was confirmation of his clarity of vision and his skill in reformulation.

Religious architecture during the Counter-Reformation

The Council of Trent was convened in 1545 by Pope Paul III as a reaction to the Lutheran and Calvinist doctrine, thus triggering a repressive artistic clampdown and causing religious buildings to be remodelled according to the precepts of the Counter-Reformation.

The regulations dictated by the clergy and officially set out in the *Instructionum Fabricae Eecclesiasticae et Suppellectilis Ecclesiasticae Libri Duo* by the Archbishop of Milan, Carlo Borromeo, published around 1577, were ushered in by the church designed by Vignola for the Jesuit Order founded by Ignatius de Loyola that became a symbol of the Counter-Reformation: the Gesù, on which construction began in 1561. The interpretation of the central liturgical theme and the diffusion of polyphonic music encouraged the building of broad, compact naves, providing a full view of the altar and ensuring excellent acoustics for the entire congregation. Furthermore, the side chapels were replaced by interconnected chapels in the Gesù. Vignola's Gesù church became a favoured model for the great city churches of reformed orders and provided the blueprint for Pellegrino Tibaldi's church of San Fedele in Milan, an undisputed monument to Carlo Borromeo's ecumenical rigour.

Palladio's two great Venetian churches, San Giorgio (begun 1565) and the Redentore (begun 1577), both conformed to the clerical regulations on religious buildings, conferring an imposing and *all'antica* feel to the basilica scheme.

**Bartolomeo Ammannati,
Villa Medici al Pincio, 1576, Rome**

The popular passion for collecting antiques satiated by the excavations that uncovered sculptures from the Roman Empire as well as other fine objects, led to an archaeologically-themed decorative trend that informed many of the architectural designs of the late cinquecento. The villa on the Pincio, built to house Ferdinando de Medici's vast collection of sculpture and antique objects, features such sumptuous ornamentation that the façade overlooking the garden constitutes a veritable collection of ancient bas-reliefs that almost dwarf the decorative classical order.

The plan of San Giorgio — which is subdivided into three functional, yet clearly distinct areas: nave and transept, presbytery and choir — was elongated in the Redentore. The basilica is characterised by generous, monumental spaces echoing the architecture of Imperial Rome. The side chapels open between the great piers of the barrel-vaulted nave, which are lit by large tripartite arched windows, borrowed from the ancient Roman *thermae*. Thus, giving the impression of a classical *aula* and accompanying the rhythmic articulation all the way up to the large bi-apsidal presbytery, which is screened from the choir by an elegant set of freestanding columns. The structural complexity of both San Giorgio and the Redentore reflect Palladio's personal interpretation of the basilica as a building typology and represent his greatest contribution to the religious architecture of the cinquecento.

Writings on architecture: treaties, manuals and compendiums

After the shattering events of the early 16th century, manuals took over from architecture as representations of the early humanist world, and, thanks to their ease of reproduction, were to prove crucial to the spread of classical Renaissance architecture throughout Europe.

The Mannerist architect, Sebastiano Serlio, published the first volume of his architectural treatise in 1537. This treatise consisted of architectural illustrations accompanied by short texts; the publication was an enormous and an immediate success. Serlio's move to France in 1541, including the accessibility of his writing, ensured that his treaty became immensely popular in France. His work had a significant influence on French architecture. Serlio's publications were translated into both French and English and were used as classical architectural handbooks by most of the leading architects at that time.

Vignola published his *Regola delli Cinque Ordini di Architettura* in 1562, as a response to the necessity to record the ancient architectural orders: their categories and constituent elements. Vignola's volume contains finely drawn

top, left
Pellegrino Tibaldi, interior of San Fedele, begun 1567, Milan

Tibaldi built the church for the Milanese Jesuit congregation to Archbishop Carlo Borromeo's specifications. The church interior, starkly classical and elegant, features a single nave articulated on either side by unusually high, monolithic Baveno marble columns, transported by river to Milan.

top, right
Andrea Palladio, San Giorgio Maggiore, begun 1565, Venice

During the second half of the cinquecento, the Council of Trent dictates determined the construction of places of worship. This resulted in a return to the basilica plan, the definitive, evolved consecration of the composite model, i.e. the fusion of a longitudinal scheme with a central space over the altar enclosed by a cupola. Palladio adhered to the new prerequisites of the counter-reformist liturgy, producing a profoundly classical church, which featured a short nave articulated by a monumental order culminating in the vertical thrust of the spatial cupola.

illustrations of the ancient orders, whilst some parts of the text consist merely of captions. Vignola's field of study was far less broad than Serlio's; he produced a kind of universal manual for the construction of architectural orders. This became a classic textbook for students of architecture during the following three centuries.

Palladio (1508–1580) took on the conception of the ancient as a philosophy for life, albeit in a profoundly different environment to that of early humanism. Palladio was taught classical studies by the erudite humanist, Giangiorgio Trissino. He grew up during the height of Vitruvius's influence, thus it was vitruvian concepts that were the guide and the theory behind his architectural œuvre. The poet, Gian Georgio Trissino, published literary works based on ancient poems and founded a learned academy in his *all'antica* villa in Cricoli, whose rooms were adorned with Greek and Latin inscriptions. Palladio's study of Roman ruins continued throughout his life; in 1556 he illustrated the edition of Vitruvius's treaty published by his patron, the erudite and learned Venetian, Daniele Barbaro. In 1570 Palladio published his famous *Quattro Libri dell'Architettura*, an academic treaty that sought to cover the entire spectrum of the art of construction. The four books contain precise and remarkably clear descriptions of the various orders along with illustrations of numerous classical and modern buildings, many of them his own work. Palladio's lucid, scientific theory of proportions based on mathematical ratios and the musical harmony of reformulated Vitruvian and Albertian principles, advocated geometric and symmetrical spatial layouts that culminate in strictly biaxial solutions. Palladio's aspirations to universal knowledge, practical skills and the ease of reproduction of the geometric plans and elevations contained in his treaty made him the most imitated architect of all time. His work was recognised throughout Europe and proved massively popular in England, particularly with architects like Inigo Jones. His four books eventually became the blueprint for 17th and 18th century European architecture.

Sebastiano Serlio, Settimo Libro delle Regole di Architettura, 1575, Ch. XLII

Sebastiano Serlio's treaty contains case studies of the various different façade typologies, including what he describes as a façade 'in the Venetian manner', characterised by loggias with triple arched trabeated openings. These façades later became known as the 'serliana'. The Serlian loggia, a device previously employed by Palladio in Veneto and Lombardy, is articulated by architectural orders that frame a central arch and two symmetrical bays, with two flat trabeations and one or more supports on either side.

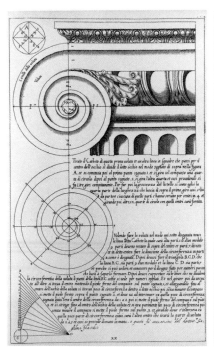

Jacopo Barozzi da Vignola, Plates XIX and XX of the *Regola delli Cinque Ordini di Architettura*, Rome, 1562

Jacopo Vignola's rigorously scientific and lucidly analytical illustrations are a testament to the tremendous cultural upheaval that marked the mid-cinquecento period. The fact that architecture was now subject to legislative norms meant that handbooks, while continuing to reformulate ancient models, had utterly changed since the days of Francesco di Giorgio and his humanist world views. The manuals were beginning to be promoted beyond Italy, making the classical ideals known throughout Europe.

GIULIO ROMANO

Federico Gonzaga's ascent to power in 1519 triggered an artistic renaissance in Mantua, spearheaded by Giulio Romano, Raphael's principal collaborator in Rome. Romano had also designed buildings in Rome, such as Palazzo Adimari Salviati, the villa for Baldassarre Turini (subsequently renamed Villa Lante) and Palazzo Stati Maccarani. One of Romano's supporters at the court of Federico Gonzaga was Baldassarre Castiglione, who had secured him his position and orchestrated his move to Mantua in 1524. Once in Mantua, Romano almost immediately rose to become a leading artist — a genuine court artist in whom Federico Gonzaga had absolute faith. Thanks to Gonzaga's patronage Romano was able to execute numerous prestigious commissions. He designed new grand residences, such as the villa at Marmirolo and Palazzo Te, as well as renovating the Gonzaga castle buildings, where he managed to achieve the ideal level of adornment and sumptuousness that the marquis desired. Romano also designed stage sets and theatrical productions, thus demonstrating the breadth of his talents. Removed from Raphael, Romano managed to develop his own individual architectural vocabulary, which, while still clearly rooted in Roman architecture, was characterised by the kind of compositional variety and attention to detail that can only be achieved with the great confidence of someone who has a profound mastery of the classical language. Romano's daring departures from the classical canon and his eccentricities became his personal cipher. Unfortunately, the commission from the Pope to take over responsibility for the complex of St Peter's in Rome, which would have been the apotheosis of his illustrious career, was thwarted by his untimely death in 1546.

**Giulio Romano,
Villa Turini Lante, c. 1521, Rome
The villa for Baldassarre**

Villa Turini was built on land once occupied by the house of Marcus Valerius Martialis, the poet commonly known as Martial. A quotation from his work is inscribed on a stone in the loggia, which exemplifies the humanist dream of building a new dwelling over the ruins of an ancient one. The orthogonal plan has a façade arranged around a double order of supports that articulate the spaces between the openings. The ground floor is characterised by Doric piers that frame the monumental arched central portal, which is flanked by half-columns and simplified windows, completed by a heavy projecting cornice. The elegant and formally decorated upper floor is subdivided by light, slightly projecting fluted Ionic pilasters and openings with banded cornices that echo the volutes of the capitals in the topmost area.

Giulio Romano, view and plan for the exterior of Palazzo Te, 1525–1535, Mantua

The grand Palazzo Gonzaga lies on Teieto island (Te) on the outskirts of Mantua on the site of an agricultural complex formerly used as stables. The layout consists of an orthogonally planned residential building with apartments grouped around a huge court-yard (without a portico) as well as a garden held by two elongated wings, terminating in a 15th century *exedra*. Romano's obvious desire to recreate an ancient villa along the lines of Villa Madama, is demonstrated by several precise elements such as the tri-partition of the main entrance, which refers to the description of the Roman atrium illustrated by Fra' Giocondo in his edition of Vitruvius's *De Architectura*. Romano reformulated the classical language of the building with rustications and deviations from the golden rule of symmetry. These unashamedly provocative violations of the norm produced syncopated rhythms in the cadence of the supports and windows, accompanied by unusual pictorial decoration.

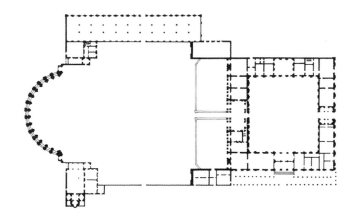

Giulio Romano, Loggia di Davide at Palazzo Te, 1525–1535, Mantua

The Loggia di Davide opens onto the translate *pescherie* and characterises the eastern elevation of the palazzo, which overlooks the garden. A double row of Doric columns with finely and richly decorated capitals supports three large *serliane* originally crowned with a rectilinear roof. The pictorial decoration on the vault and lunettes features scenes from the life of David and was eventually completed in 1532, shortly before the arrival of Emperor Charles V of Hapsburg on his second visit to Mantua.

The arrival of this powerful ruler in the small duchy ignited a decorative programme intended to fuse the iconographic and symbolic decoration of Palazzo Te with that of an imperial palace worthy of the triumphs of Federico and his large court.

MICHELANGELO/ROME UNDER POPE PAUL III

Cardinal Alessandro Farnese's election to the Pontificate in 1534 heralded a new era for Rome after the deep humiliation and the grave cultural and political crisis wrought by the Sack of Rome in 1527.

Pope Paul III instigated a new programme of church renovation and restoration, which also served to flaunt the power and influence of the House of Farnese. Once again, Rome became the chosen destination for architects wishing to study the ruins there and to become employed in the many new building projects.

Pirro Ligorio, the Zuccari brothers, Vignola and Palladio were all based in Rome during this particular period, where they set new architectural trends that strove to reconcile humanist dictates with the rigorous approach ordered by the Council of Trent. The council was established in 1545 by Pope Paul III to re-enforce the fundamental tenets of the Roman Catholic Church.

The Pope's plan for the urban rehabilitation of the city took precedence over the refurbishment of the enormous family palazzo. Antonio da Sangallo the Younger was commissioned to design the, as-yet, unbuilt parts of the palazzo and to open up a square in front of the building, which involved demolition on a huge scale. Michelangelo moved to Rome in 1534 and was employed officially by the Pontiff the following year when he executed *The Last Judgement* in the Sistine Chapel. Subsequent to Sangallo's death in 1546, Michelangelo became chief architect at St Peter's Basilica and Palazzo Farnese which, along with the restructuring of the Campidoglio, kept him occupied until his death in 1564.

opposite page
Michelangelo Buonarroti, cupola of St Peter's Basilica, Rome

The exterior of Michelangelo's building features a single order of giant Corinthian pilasters that articulate the enormous vertical thrust and set the scene for the steep ascent above the internal crossing. The enormous dome rises from the perimeter wall of the building, its apertures alternating with pairs of columns standing proud of the building, extending into the trabeation and the ribs of the cupola, thereby signifying the construction method. Its obvious geometric derivation from Brunelleschi's cupola is translated into an imposing, plastic and carefully modelled dome, invested with sculptural monumentality. Michelangelo's design, which was revolutionary compared with the other post-Bramante solutions, laid the foundation for Maderno and Bernini's projects, which brought work on the basilica to a definitive conclusion.

Michelangelo Buonarroti and Antonio da Sangallo the Younger, courtyard of Palazzo Farnese, begun 1546, Rome

Michelangelo was commissioned to work on the areas of Palazzo Farnese that had remained unfinished after the death of Sangallo. These areas were concentrated on the garden side of the building: the enormous window on the façade and the completion of the two upper storeys with their heavy cornice. Michelangelo added a frieze to the central level, which Antonio had already built. Michelangelo also redesigned the architectural decoration on the top floor, with Corinthian pilasters projecting from half-pilasters. Michelangelo's novel vocabulary was a significant departure from the purity of ancient classical architecture and was saturated with structurally plastic modelling. He also shaped the elaborate fenestration, paving the way for the developments of the late cinquecento.

REM·PRINCIPIS·APOST PAVLVS·V·BVRGHESIVS·ROM

left
Michelangelo Buonarroti and Giacomo della Porta, Palazzo dei Conservatori, 1630s, Rome

Michelangelo succeeded in visually unifying the elevations on the square with his masterful use of the giant order that articulates the façades of Palazzo dei Conservatori, Palazzo Nuovo and Palazzo Senatorio. The front elevation of Palazzo dei Conservatori, which was completed by Giacomo della Porta, features an architraved portico on the ground floor with free Ionic columns intersected with a monumental order of Corinthian pilasters. The larger order articulates the openings on both floors and rises up to the heavy cornice, creating a solemn and imposing effect.

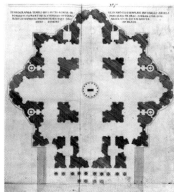

Stefano Dupérac, plan of St Peter's according to a design by Michelangelo

Michelangelo's arrival at the St Peter's complex marked a paradigm shift in building operations, triggering the departure of Antonio da Sangallo's assistants and the demolition of the southern hemicycle of the basilica, which had been built by Raphael and Sangallo in 1519. Michelangelo's plan layout was based on the existing structures of the ancient choir and provided for a return to the ancient centralised quincunx scheme. This was, however, a complete reversal of Bramante's first version. Michelangelo simplified the immense basilica imagined by Sangallo and laid out, rather, a scheme in which the pure Greek cross emerges from a square formed by the spaces around the great diagonal piers.

VASARI/FLORENCE UNDER COSIMO I

The rise to power of Cosimo de' Medici, son of Giovanni dalle Bande Nere and niece of Lorenzo il Magnifico, in 1537, triggered a renaissance in Florentine art that corresponded to his absolutist aspirations. The nobleman saw the renovation of the city as being symbolic of his own triumph and that of his family. In practical terms, building renewal in Florence was achieved through the *bando* (call for tenders) issued by Cosimo in 1551, which authorised the expropriation of houses and land in order to make way for new buildings worthy of Grand duke Florence. Cosimo's desire to reflect the grandeur of the House of Medici in a Florentine architectural style typical of the Medici's came to fruition in the early 1550s through his artistic collaboration with Giorgio Vasari who, along with Bartolomeo Ammannati and Bernardo Buontalenti, remodelled the face of Florence, interpreting the aspirations of both the court and the Grandduke himself. Vasari, born in Arezzo in 1511, was greatly influenced by Michelangelo and was responsible for organising and orchestrating Michelangelo's funeral in 1564. Vasari, a true Renaissance man, was a sculptor, painter and architect; his tireless devotion to Cosimo exemplifies the ideal artist, versatile and practical, without whom the establishment of the State would have been far more difficult. Cosimo's requisition of Palazzo della Signoria, later Palazzo Vecchio, for his courtly residence as well as the subsequent building of the Uffizi set the seal on his absolute supremacy and, with Vasari's help, he transformed the heart of Florentine civil institutions into a hub of Medici power.

Giorgio Vasari, Salone dei Cinquecento in Palazzo Vecchio, begun 1555, Florence

The need for a more representative royal palace prompted Cosimo to abandon his residence on Via Larga in 1540 in favour of the 14th century Palazzo della Signoria. Cosimo embarked upon a major restructuring programme designed to turn the palazzo into a grand Medici residence. The medieval exterior was left intact by the architect and was offset by the wonderful interior decoration: stuccoes and frescoes proclaiming the glory of Florence and the Grandduke himself. The most challenging task was the renovation of the Salone dei Cinquecento, created by Cronaca in 1494 and remodelled by Vasari on the occasion of the marriage of Cosimo's heir, Francesco, to Joan, daughter of the Austrian Emperor. Vasari's skills could be fully appreciated in this palazzo. He raised the ceiling by seven metres and adorned it with sumptuous decoration of gilded coffers.

Giorgio Vasari, elevation, plan and detail from the façade of the Palazzo degli Uffizi, 1560, Florence

Cosimo's commission for the Palazzo degli Uffizi, destined to house the city's administrative and judicial *Magistrature*, was geared to ensuring that the substantial funds and fierce autonomies of the new republican institutions remained under ducal control. The decision to site the building near the seat of political power, alongside the River Arno, was by no means coincidental. The design culminated in an elongated building block consisting of functional units ('uffizi' or offices) placed alongside one another. The spatial module corresponding to each office was echoed on the exterior of the building into a tripartite bay, with cruciform piers framing three trabeated columns.

Giorgio Vasari, Palazzo degli Uffizi, 1560, Florence

This enormous building, almost 150 metres in length, consists of two wings with different plan footprints sited parallel to one another to form a narrow arcaded square terminating at the River Arno with a screen created by a double order of *serliane*.

The decision to choose an elongated volume meant that the irregularity of the wings behind could be maintained, leading to savings in time and construction costs compared with the costs of constructing a block and courtyard. Departing from the canonical Renaissance palazzo layout indicates Vasari's pragmatic approach and his lucid compositional freedom. The articulation of the elevations, in typically Brunelleschian duotone, owes a great deal also to Michelangelo's vocabulary, creating a style of architecture drawn from the supreme models of Florentine culture. The short river frontage, which partly encloses the long, narrow square, establishes a visual link between the political hub of Piazza della Signoria, the river and the hills on the far side, whilst also acting as a prelude to the Corridoio Vasariano, the elevated walkway that curves through the city to connect to Palazzo Vecchio with the Pitti Palace.

AMMANNATI AND BUONTALENTI

Bartolomeo Ammannati (1511–1592) was invited back to Florence by Vasari (with whom he had previously worked in 1555 on Villa Giulia in Rome) corresponded to the start of Cosimo I's great urban remodelling plans. A pupil of Bandinelli and Jacopo Sansovino, Ammannati was an architect and a sculptor, whose many works combined classicism with a distinctly unfettered experimentation. Ammannati completed the vestibule in the Biblioteca Laurenziana in Florence to Michelangelo's plans and received a great many commissions from the wealthy bourgeois and provincial patrons circulating the Medici court. He was a great supporter of Cosimo I's ambitious renovation plans for the city, spearheading a propaganda campaign that was to change the face of Florence forever.

Bernardo Buontalenti (1536–1608) took over from Vasari at the Uffizi in 1574, employing his skills as a military engineer in the renovation of the Duchy's defences and in the expansion plans for the city of Leghorn, which involved the construction of pentagonal city fortification walls.

bottom, left
Bartolomeo Ammannati, front elevation of the Cortile degli Svizzeri, Palazzo Pubblico, 1576, Lucca

Palazzo Pubblico in Lucca, damaged by the explosion in the Torre delle Polveri in 1576, was reconstructed by Bartolomeo Ammannati into two blocks orientated onto a large courtyard.

The façade of the palazzo, which opens onto a courtyard, has aedicules on the first floor, surmounted by tablets adorned with plant and animal motifs. The elevations on the upper floor are articulated by rectangular windows that alternate with wide *serliane*, a characteristic and recurrent motif in Ammannati's architectural vocabulary.

opposite page, right
Bernardo Buontalenti, Grotto Grande, Boboli Gardens, begun 1583, Florence

The Grotta Grande, built by Vasari into the lower section of the façade, owes its extraordinary appearance to Bernardo Buontalenti, who started work on it in 1583. The artificial grotto contains an eloquent combination of architecture, painting and sculpture on the theme of amorphous matter and natural chaos, which achieves order and harmony through metamorphosis. The opposing forces of nature and art versus chaos and harmony, typical of the ideas of the alchemists in which Grandduke Francesco I was so greatly interested, translate into an exuberant and Mannerist decoration within the grotto, where disorder is manifest in the accretions that overrun the space and flow like primordial lava. Inside the grotto, where Michelangelo's *Prisoners* had previously stood, the sculptures and decorations provided a backdrop to the, now, invisible fountains, creating a symbolic mise-en-scène.

Bartolomeo Ammannati, Palazzo Pitti courtyard, begun 1560, Florence

The design for the enormous palazzo, which was owned by Luca Pitti, was attributed to Brunelleschi. Remaining incomplete on Pitti's death, it was later radically extended from 1549 onwards, when it became the second court residence. Ammannati, who took over responsibility for the building works from Vasari in 1560, added two new wings to the central block, which he attached to the corners of the existing building, thus almost doubling its volume. He also added a huge courtyard, which opens out over the magnificent Boboli Gardens to the rear. The new stone façade of the back elevation is starkly rusticated, bringing the half-columns on the first floor closer to one another, but reducing into sculptural, horizontal *fasciae* on the two upper floors, to create a stone and structural configuration reminiscent of Sansovino's Zecca project.

JACOPO BAROZZI DA VIGNOLA

In 1550 Vignola left Bologna, resigned his position as chief architect at the basilica of San Petronio and moved to Rome to work for Giovanni Maria del Monte, who had been elected to the pontificate as Pope Julius III. The two men had met several years earlier when the Cardinal was Pope's Legate in Bologna, which was the second most important city in the Pontifical State territories. Vignola's first work for the Pope was a prestigious commission for a sumptuous suburban villa outside Rome, where Pope Julius intended to house his vast collection of antiques. Construction of the villa started in 1550. Vignola's considerable professional skills, a combination of technical ability and lucid mastery of formal syntax, ensured that he rose rapidly to the top of the architectural ranks in Rome and the Papal States, securing prestigious commissions, such as the completion of Palazzo Farnese in Rome. The commission for the villa was granted by the Cardinals, Alessandro and Ranuccio, nephews of Pope Paul III, who favoured Vignola as their architect. After Ranuccio's death in 1565, Alessandro Farnese, an extremely powerful and ambitious cardinal in the Roman Curia, sponsored all Vignola's most important and best-known works. These included: the magnificent residence in Caprarola, the palazzo in Piacenza and the church of the Gesù. The publication, in 1562, of the *Regola delli Cinque Ordini d'Architettura*, which was an immediate and well-deserved success, set the seal on Vignola's illustrious career. Vignola died in 1573 and was buried in the temple to distinguished men, namely, the Pantheon.

Jacopo Barozzi da Vignola, Sant'Andrea in Via Flaminia, 1552–1553, Rome

Vignola designed the church as a commission from Pope Julius III, near the Pope's villa. The church consists of a small rectangular space with a *scarsella*, or flat pedimented temple shape, running the length of the short elevation of the building. The formal simplicity of the plan is offset by the revolutionary oval cupola, which rises from elliptical pendentives in a radical blend of traditional longitudinal and humanist, centrally-planned scheme. The elliptical shape of the cupola, destined to become a popular feature of 17th century architecture, is also visible on the outside of the building. The high dome is articulated with an ancient-style heavy cornice and graded roof covering. The external ancient appearance is emphasised by the formality of the façade, which features tall Corinthian pilasters supporting a tympanum and an attic, as with a classical pronaos modelled on the Pantheon.

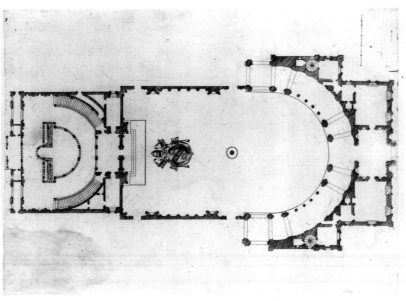

Jacopo Barozzi da Vignola and Bartolomeo Ammannati, view of the façade and plan of Villa Giulia, begun 1550, Rome

Vignola's project for Pope Julius III's residence on the outskirts of Rome (which was replanned and partly altered by subsequent interventions by Vasari and Ammannati) creates a succession of open spaces along a longitudinal axis that terminates with the villa itself, configured behind a large *exedra* orientated towards the city. There is a tripartite arch over the central bay of the façade, enclosing the monumental entrance, which provides the vanishing point for the entire project. The rustication demarking the corners and the aedicule-type structure of the main entrance, which stand out against the plastered walls, are motifs drawn from Sangallo's Palazzo Farnese, though here Vignola has translated them into his own personal, formal language.

THE MASTERPIECE
PALAZZO FARNESE, CAPRAROLA

The Farnese family fiefdom of Caprarola, a small town sixty miles from Rome, was already the location of a fortress — begun in 1520 but never completed — by Antonio da Sangallo the Younger and Baldassare Peruzzi. In 1559, under orders from Cardinal Alessandro Farnese, who wished to make it his country seat, Vignola commenced with the renovation of the pentagonal building, with its massive corner bastions. The absolute power wielded over the town by the Farnese nobleman is embodied by the dominant and commanding position of the fortress above the town, its silhouette standing boldly out at the culmination of a lengthy climb carved out of the medieval urban fabric. Vignola used his extraordinary talent as an architect to transform the military building into a sumptuous and monumental villa, with open-air terraces rather than bastions and two orders of Ionic and composite pilasters framing and structuring the severe exterior. The magnificent circular courtyard at the centre of the pentagon, which has simple rustic arcades on the ground floor and first floor arcades framed by pairs of Ionic columns, echoes Bramante's classical designs for Palazzo Caprini and the Belvedere. The plan groups together the opulently decorated rooms by Taddeo, Zuccari, Bertoia and Vignola.

The striking entrance to the villa is situated above two broad terraces accessed by two monumental staircases: one pincer-shaped with two semi-circular flights of broad, shallow steps and the other a double rectilinear staircase modelled on the stairway in the Belvedere courtyard. Two smaller floors above the loggia on the *piano nobile* are articulated by Ionic pilasters. These levels were utilised by family and staff, linked by a single composite order.

opposite page
Jacopo Barozzi da Vignola, spiral staircase at Palazzo Farnese, 1559, Caprarola, Viterbo

Vignola's design for Caprarola borrows several details from Bramanate's Belvedere, which he employed in the outside stairway, the composition of the courtyard and also in the spectacular spiral staircase that links the different levels of the palazzo. The paired Doric columns support the trabeation, which, in turn, acts as the base for the uppermost flight of stairs. The compositional sophistication of the space is enriched by frescoes of grotesques on the walls and a vault which creates an eloquent grandeur.

THE ITALIAN GARDEN

The Renaissance park or *'barco'*, had its origins in the hunting traditions of the aristocracy. When the classical villa came back into fashion during the late quattrocento, it became common practice to set aside part of the hunting grounds for an ornamental garden for the purposes of contemplation and re-laxation. Bramante's Belvedere, the successful Villa Madama, Villa Giulia and Palazzo Farnese set the trend for architects to conceive gardens as part of the natural environment. However, they were to be subjected to the rules of geometry, order and proportion. Country houses opened out into loggias and courtyards framed in perspective by the architecture of the surrounding gar-dens, where water features and fountains created the scenic, spectacular mises-en-scène of noble prestige. From the mid-cinquecento onwards the Italian garden became a popular feature, particularly for the area around Rome and was testament to the ostentatious ambitions of the powerful car-dinals in the Roman Curia, who commissioned opulent residences set in the centre of large, manicured gardens. By the turn of the century, the concept of the planned park had been exported all over Europe, giving rise to the 'Italian' garden, a spectacular crown to royal palaces. It was only with the fall of the an-cien régime and the birth of the landscaped garden that the popularity of the architectural Italian garden began to decline.

Jacopo Barozzi da Vignola, Palazzo Farnese at Caprarola, Viterbo, front view section and plan (bottom right) of Villa d'Este at Tivoli and water features on lateral axis (left), Rome

Pirro Logorio built the villa at Tivoli in 1550, as a commission from Cardinal Ippolito d'Este of Ferrara, who desired a residence worthy of his status in Rome, where he was governor-elect. The programme provided for the ren-ovation and extension of the pre-existing Benedictine monastery and the creation of a huge garden with terraces, focused on a central axis, which framed the main entrance to the building. The reclamation of the land, which already seemed to have been a monumental task in itself, set the stage for a magnificent, theatrical garden design, where fountains and water features played central roles.

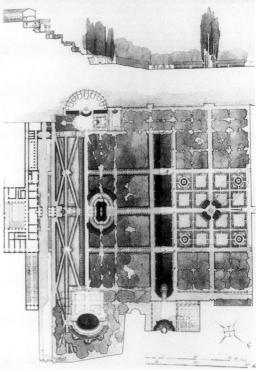

Garden at Villa Lante, begun 1566, Bagnaia, Viterbo

The 'barco', or park, at Bagnaia, where the bishops of Viterbo chose to spend their holidays, was created for Cardinale Raffaele Riario in 1514.

Giovan Francesco Gambaro, Bishop of Viterbo since 1566, embarked on the remodelling of Villa Lante and its grounds during the 1570s. The bishop entrusted the design of the garden to Tommaso Ghinucci, a hydraulic engineer and garden designer who had previously worked on the villa at Tivoli.

Compared with Villa d'Este, the quadrangular garden space, symmetrical to the built structures, was revolutionary. The garden at Bagnaia is narrower and therefore favours a longitudinal axis, 230 metres long; the garden is thus split into three large square *parterres* that create distinct areas. On arrival, visitors are overwhelmed by the extraordinary vision before them, which is amplified by four sculptural basins grouped around a monumental circular fountain at the end of the garden. The second *parterre*, which contains two twin *casini*, or follies, leads to the upper level, which is adorned with statuary and *capricci* with flights of steps running parallel to a central water basin that feeds into the Fontana dei Delfini and, higher still, into the spectacular Fontana del Deluvio, a deep rocky artificial basin flanked by sculptures of giants' heads.

THE CHURCH AND THE COUNTER-REFORMATION

The dogmatic change of course ordered by the Roman Catholic Church, sanctioned by the Council of Trent, which erupted as the Counter-Reformation, required the clergy to sieze control of liturgical design. This change had a significant impact on the structural configuration of churches during the second half of the 16th century. The central role of prayer and the congregation's choral participation in the mass led to a revision of the longitudinal plan, which was characterised by a wide *aula*-type nave with intersecting side chapels designed to prevent the liturgical rites being disturbed. The many religious buildings produced during this period in line with Counter-Reformist dictates were frequently decorated in the Baroque style at a later date. An example of this is the church of the Gesù, where the original appearance, stark and spare and rigidly articulated by architectural orders, was later completely altered. The new architectural rules were to be officially sanctioned by the Archbishop of Milan, Carlo Borromeo, in his *Instructionum Fabricae Ecclesiasticae et Suppellectilis Ecclesiasticae Libri Duo*, published c. 1577, which applied the Tridentine Council principles to eccumenical buildings. The ultimate example of the application of the new rules was the Gesù church, the founding church of the Society of Jesus, which was built to a design by Jacopo Barozzi da Vignola from 1561 and was completed in the early 1570s with a façade by Giacomo della Porta. Gesù became the prototype for churches of the Counter-Reformation.

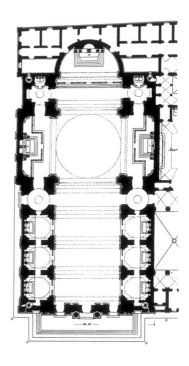

Giacomo della Porta,
Church of the Gesù, 1571, Rome

Alessandro Farnese rejected Vignola's 1571 design for the façade in favour of one by the younger architect, Giacomo della Porta. The front elevation has superimposed orders standing proud on the central axis, which is further emphasised by the monumentality of the large aedicule framing the entrance, containing a marble crest and a Christogram carved by Bartolomeo.

Jacopo Barozzi da Vignola, interior of the Church of the Gesù, 1561, Rome, and plan of the Church of the Gesù (opposite page, top), P. M. Letarouilly, *Edifices de Rome Moderne*, Paris, 1868–1874

The first project by Nanni di Baccio Bigi for the new church for the Society of Jesus dates back to 1550 and is evidence that the Order intended to build a church with an immense nave even at that early stage. The project was finally realised in 1561, when Alessandro Farnese became the Society's patron. Farnese agreed to finance the building and entrusted the project to his favourite architect, Vignola. The architect's plan features a 5.5-metre-wide nave that opens out into four interconnecting chapels on either side, which are partly covered by small oval cupolas. An elongated gallery above the chapels leads onto the nave and is pierced with *coretti*, openings covered with grilles through which the brothers were able to take part privately in the services. The huge *tribuna*, compressed in width, is part of the huge *aula* that forms the building interior and conforms to a centralised quincunx plan, where the central cupola is joined by four smaller cupolas over the chapels situated on the diagonals. The church of Sant'Andrea in Mantua was the inspiration for the barrel vault, which is supported by paired pilasters rising up from the chapel openings. In the Church of the Gesù, Alberti's monolithic granite structure is translated into an open ceiling pierced with lunettes which allow light to enter the building, articulating the longitudinal rhythm and emphasising the central core of the presbytery.

JACOPO SANSOVINO IN VENICE

The Florentine, Jacopo Tatti (1486–1570), a pupil of the sculptor, Andrea Sansovino, whose name he adopted, worked for a lengthy period in Rome, where he learnt the language of classical architecture from Giuliano da Sangallo firstly and, later, from Raphael, Sangallo the Younger, Peruzzi and Romano; all artists who claimed Bramante's legacy as their own. Sansovino arrived in Venice in August 1527, fleeing the Sack of Rome and was appointed *Proto della Repubblica* (Chief Architect of the Republic) two years later. This was an extremely prestigious position, which placed him at the realm of Venice's urban planning and public architecture development. The powers vested in him by Doge Andre Gritti, as well as the major expropriation of buildings around St Mark's Square enabled Sansovino to embark on an ambitious urban renovation plan for the centre of Venice, at the hub of the city's public and religious institutions. Sansovino's programme, which included building the Zecca, the Libreria Marciana and the Loggetta, involved the architectural remodelling of the two porticoed piazzas into what was to become a monumental complex in the medieval urban fabric. The Zecca, the Libreria and the Ducal Palace, along with the Procuratie complex, are all buildings with colonnades and without determining axes. They create the backdrop for the basilica, the bell-tower and the Loggetta buildings that all form part of an urban theatre where the old and the new dovetail harmoniously.

opposite page, top
Jacopo Sansovino, Zecca, 1536, Venice

The Zecca, the new city mint, was built along the San Marco quay; with its heavy rustication it looks as if it could be a fortress for the Serenissima. The lower floor — devoid of orders — has rustic arches with alternate protruding blocks of ashlar, which serve to increase the plastic, chiaroscuro effect of the surface. The two upper registers are articulated by tall, ringed Doric and Ionic half-columns, which offset the windows. The openings on the central floor are surmounted by a double projecting lintol that underscores the sense of horizontal stability and is held above the columns immediately below the capital, making the shafts look as though they are tapered, which is not in fact the case.

Jacopo Sansovino,
Palazzo Corner, begun 1545, Venice

The palazzo was designed during the 1530s, but building did not start until later, in 1545. As is the case in the Zecca, the structure is held on a rusticated plinth, with protruding blocks of ashlar stone. The triple-arched portico, accessed by a flight of steps, was inspired by the north entrance of Palazzo Te in Mantua and is flanked by gable-topped windows framed by Doric half-columns. The elongated, elegant brackets above define the apertures on the mezzanine floor and echo designs by Romano and Michelangelo. The two upper orders, configured in the manner of the traditionally reworked Colosseum and the Theatre of Marcellus, are characterised by pairs of half-columns that flank the sides of the apertures, emphasising the substantial plasticity of the façade. The reinterpretation of the Venetian architectural typology, which provides for a large *sala* rather than a *peristylium*, is scarcely perceptible in the three clustered, central openings of the great *salone*.

Jacopo Sansovino, Loggetta, 1537, Venice

This small loggia, built at the base of St Mark's bell-tower is characterised by four sets of paired columns framing an equal number of niches, alternating with three large apertures. A high attic is situated above the entablature, which is adorned with bas-relief panels illustrating the story of the Serenissima. The formal configuration of the Loggetta draws on a project for the façade of San Lorenzo in Florence by Giuliano da Sangallo, a fellow citizen and patron of Sansovino's when Sangallo first went to Rome.

SANMICHELI IN VERONA

Michele Sanmicheli (1487/8–1559) was born into a family of stonemasons in Verona, to where he returned after a lengthy period in Rome and Orvieto, where he supervised the building works on the Duomo. Sanmicheli's skill as a military architect, which Vasari ascribed to his knowledge of the fortifications for Pope Clement VII, led to his becoming a military engineer in the service of the Venetian Republic and to his return to Verona in 1526. His mastery of the *all'antica* lexicon and familiarity with the ancient Roman classical culture at the turn of the century made him, along with Jacopo Sansovino, one of the principal proponents of classical Vitruvian language and precepts in the Veneto. Sanmicheli's methods of reworking the classical conventions were informed by his own experience and were also deeply influenced by the many Roman ruins in Verona, which contained nearly as many intact Roman remains as in Rome. The arena, the theatre, Porta Borsari and Porta Leoni, the Gavi Arch and the Jupiter Ammone Arch, along with the Roman ruins, became Sanmicheli's architectural frame of reference. Furthermore, due to a loose interpretation of an inscription on the Gavi Arch, Verona had traditionally been held to be the birthplace of Vitruvius, the ultimate tutor of Renaissance architects and the prominent architect of ancient Roman buildings.

**Michele Sanmicheli,
Palazzo Bevilacqua, 1530s, Verona**

Palazzo Bevilacqua, commissioned by the powerful family at the helm one of Verona's major political factions, is believed to have been erected in the early 1530s. The façade, which replaced a pre-existing wall that encircled the property, was originally designed to have fifteen bays rather than the seven which were actually built. The façade was intended to serve as a monumental expression of the prestige and power of the Bevilacqua family. The complex rhythms of the magnificent façade are expressed in the articulation of the apertures and supports on both levels. The ground floor, resting on a rustic base, features Doric pilasters alternating with large and small arches, which attempt to maintain the same opening dimension. A similar device is used for the upper area, where the elegant Corinthian order frames windows with large and small arches, unified by the rectangular apertures inside the imposts. The elegant columns maintain their own rhythm, determined by the directions of the fluting on the column shafts.

**Michele Sanmicheli, Palazzo
Canossa, 1526–1528, Verona**

The palazzo, built for Bishop Lodovico
Canossa between 1526 and 1528,
shares some *all'antica* features with
Roman palazzi of the same period,
which were derived from Vitruvius's
ancient house. The tripartite, rectangular layout has a double row of
rooms grouped around a courtyard,
which is accessed through an atrium
and a vestibule.The façade, once completely adorned with frescoes, consist
of two orders, it has a rustic plinth
surmounted by paired pilasters, as in
Bramante's popular design for
Palazzo Caprini. The capitals in the
courtyard, however, are inspired by
Veronese antiquities, drawn from the
Roman theatre and amphitheatre.

ANDREA PALLADIO

Andrea della Gondola, the son of a miller, was born in Padua in 1508. He moved with his family to Vicenza in 1534, where he worked as a stonemason in the city's most highly regarded workshop. The wealthy Vicentine ruling classes, who were cultured and wanted renewal, as well as his contact with the great architectural heirs of Roman classicism, Sansovino, Serlio and Sanmicheli in Venice and Romano in Mantua, played a fundamental role in Palladio's meteoric rise. His unusual talent, based on ancient ideals, found its ideal nurturing place in the enlightened society of Vicenza where he was taken under the wing by the literary humanist, Giangiorgio Trissino, who gave him the name 'Palladio' inspired by Greek mythology. His early exposure to Rome in the 1540s and his involvement with the building of the great Palazzo Thiene, designed by Giulio Romano (which Palladio later supervised after Romano's death in 1546) marked a turning point in his artistic maturity, leading to his commissions for the town hall in Vicenza and to a great number of private commissions. Palladio's collaboration with the humanist, Daniele Barbaro — one of the cinquecento's more eclectic characters — was a driving force. The two men worked together on the Villa in Maser as well as on Palladio's illustrations for Barbaro's edition of Vitruvius, published in 1556. Barbaro's classical knowledge and in-depth exploration of ancient architecture and Vitruvius's writings formed the basis for Palladio's architectural output and for his publication of *Quattro Libri dell'Architectura* in 1570, a manual containing illustrations of ancient and modern buildings, as well as illustrations his own work, which proved extremely successful.

Andrea Palladio, Basilica, begun 1549, Vicenza

The exterior of the 15th century Palazzo della Ragione, which had once hosted meetings of the town council, collapsed in 1496. The serious structural problems and the irregularity of the internal layout were brilliantly solved by Palladio's use of the *serliana* in a double *all'antica* loggia on two floors of the basilica. The space between the columns and the piers manages to compensate for the differing width dimensions of the bays. The *serliana* motif, which derives from the ancient Arch at Aquino, was already familiar to Giuliano and Antonio da Sangallo and was also employed by Romano and Sansovino. Palladio's reinterpretation of it here, however, achieved a completely new, solemn monumentality, creating a sombre structure decorated soberly. This solemnity contributed to the popularity of the basilica as a prototype.

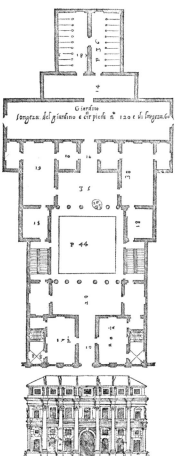

Andrea Palladio, Palazzo Valmarana, 1565, Vicenza, view (left), plan and elevation (right) Andrea Palladio, *I Quattro Libri dell'Architettura*, Venice 1570, II.

Palladio experimented with the simultaneous use of a giant order of pilasters that articulates the entire front of the façade of Palazzo Valmarana, continuing all the way up to the heavy cornice and a minor order, which frames the apertures on the lower floor. The use of the double-intersected-order motif, also employed in Palladian churches of the same period, had a precedent in Michelangelo's Palazzo dei Conservatori on the Capitoline Hill. The plan of the palazzo, which has a double row of perfectly symmetrical spaces overlooking the courtyard, is testament to the requirement to keep the habitation within the confines of the massive block, a common challenge for palazzi built along the street edge.

VILLAS

The crisis in Venetian maritime trade, triggered by the new Atlantic routes and the country's growing reliance on its own agricultural produce, was responsible for the great burgeoning of residential Venetian dwellings during the cinquecento period. Unlike Roman and Tuscan villas of the same era, these Villas were also used for agricultural purposes. Cultured and wealthy clients in Vicenza, Verona and Venice were eager to build rural villas surrounded by rolling estates for practical and functional reasons. They families were also motivated by the desire to live in a noble and dignified manner, following the *all'antica* precepts that elevated country residences to the status of classical villas. Palladio was responsible for fulfilling this desire, designing a plethora of villas involving numerous symmetrical and axial variations of formal classical configurations to suit the specific agricultural needs of his patrons. The Palladian residences, designed according to Vitruvian symmetrical and proportional dictates, are based on square or rectangular plans, with rooms grouped around a large, central double-volume hall. The villa block, which was often extended with wings intended for agricultural use, known as *barchesse*, is ennobled by the addition of a classical pronaos on the façade that is characteristic of all Palladio's villas in their various forms. The formal elegance of the Palladian villas soon became the model of choice for British architects, whose infinite reproductions of Palladio's compositional plans resulted in the enormous success of his style abroad, in both England and America.

Andrea Palladio, Villa Barbaro, 1550–1560, Maser, Treviso

Villa Barbaro in Maser was built for Daniele Barbaro, patriarch of Aquileia and his brother Marcantonio, the Venetian ambassador between 1550 and 1560. The following of humanist culture by his clients, coupled with their great wealth, enabled Palladio to create one of his most imposing buildings. The magnificent architecture acts as backdrop to the stucco decorations by Alessandro Vittoria and to the painted frescoes by Paolo Veronese. The layout of the villa, clearly inspired by the Baths of Diocletian, consists of two juxtaposed elements: the residential block, which projects out over the garden with a classical pronaos, and the elongated lateral *barchesse* with open arcades and animal stables. The rear of the building features a *nymphaeum* with statues of pagan gods by Vittoria.

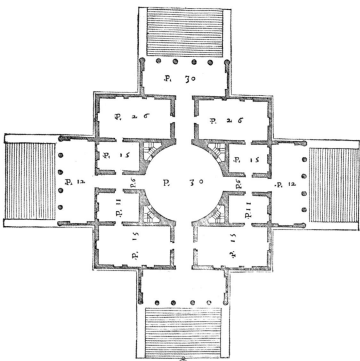

Andrea Palladio, La Rotonda, begun 1566, Vicenza (top) and plan (left) by A. Palladio, I Quattro Libri dell'Architettura, Venice, 1570

La Rotonda was built for Paolo Almerico, a priest in the Roman Curia, who was returning to Vicenza on his retirement. The residence thus has no agricultural function and is simply a rural dwelling built for a life of refinement and contemplation. The villa was designed to relate harmoniously with the surrounding countryside. The layout of the villa is testament to Palladio's firm commitment to Vitruvian centrality and symmetry. It is built according to a symmetrical, square plan, with a circular central hall covered with a dome, from which the secondary spaces open, with four identical modular units along the two orthogonal axes. The axial formality also applies to the exterior of the building.

Andrea Palladio, Villa Foscari also known as La Malcontenta, c. 1559, Mira, Venice

The residence built for the Venetian brothers, Nicolò and Alvise Foscari, stands on the periphery of the Lagoon, along the Brenta River. The suburban villa is easily accessible by boat from the city centre. The geometric block has been built onto a high plinth in order to keep out the damp, but also gives the villa the appearance of a majestic ancient temple. The hexastyle pronaos that structures the main façade, flanked by the twin access steps to the loggia, is reminiscent of the classical *tempietto* at the mouth of the Clitumno River, which was well known to Palladio. The villa demonstrates Palladio's considerable skills in designing and building great monumental architecture despite having to use cheap materials such as brick, which he used to build most of the structural parts of the villa, including the columns. In order to make the masonry look like *all'antica* stone decoration Palladio covered the brickwork with Marmorino plaster.

bottom, right
Andrea Palladio, Villa Sarego, c. 1565, Santa Sofia di Pedemonte, Verona, plan and elevation by A. Palladio, *I Quattro Libri dell'Architettura*, 1570

Villa Sarego was built by Palladio for Marcantonio Sarego of Verona and is unique in the repertoire of Palladian villas. This unique quality is due, partly, to its outlying position to the west of Verona and also due to the expressive interpretation of the massive columnation. Only a small portion of the villa was actually built, however the design was nevertheless familiar thanks to drawings by Palladio. The villa had the rare distinction of being arranged around an enormous central courtyard, which was modelled on reconstructed Vitruvian buildings. The massive remaining structures, hewn from stone from the nearby quarry of his client are defined by the superimposition of rustically carved stone, rows of irregular columns that lend an entirely new expressive and sculptural dynamic to the building, reminiscent of the work of Michelangelo.

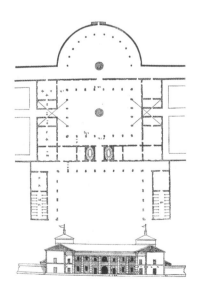

THE MASTERPIECE
THE TEATRO OLIMPICO, OLYMPIC THEATRE, VICENZA

Palladio's design for the Teatro Olimpico was commissioned by a group of intellectual Vicentine aristocrats, who wanted to build an *all'antica* theatre inside a pre-existing medieval complex that would be of an equivalent architectural standard as their splendid dwellings in the 'Little Rome' that Vicenza had become. The Accademia Olimpica, established in 1555 by some enlightened members of the nobility, including Palladio himself, was set up to spread and cultivate the arts, the sciences and mathematics in particular. It was this academy that promoted the building of a theatre in 1579 and the members also helped to finance the project. Portraits of the academics thus appear on the theatre's sculptured busts, attired like actors and spectators of ancient times. Constructing the Teatro Olimpico ab-sorbed the final months of Palladio's life after his final return to his Vicentine residence from Venice, where he had been based since around 1570. Building had only just begun on the theatre at the time of his death, in 1580. Fortunately the wealth of documentation he left behind enabled his son, Silla, to continue with the project, which was completed a few years later with Vincenzo Scamozzi's timber stage set. The Teatro Olimpico is a reconstruction of the ancient theatre as described by Vitruvius. It is inspired by some still intact Roman examples and is a profoundly archaeological work, far removed from his other contemporary theatres, where the function as theatre was given secondary place whilst philology and classical theorising of the academics were placed first.

Andrea Palladio and Vincenzo Scamozzi, stage set for the Teatro Olimpico, begun 1580, Vicenza

The three-dimensional scale of the theatre, built by Vincenzo Scamozzi in 1585, was a departure from the two-dimensional painted backdrop, which first appeared in the early cinquecento, usually depicting an urban or pastoral scene. The rectangular proscenium of the Teatro Olimpico features a large central arch, flanked by two sets of smaller rectangular doorways, which lead into seven city streets bordered by classical façades.

THE MASTERPIECE
SAN GIORGIO AND THE REDENTORE IN VENICE

Andrea Palladio, façade and floor plan for San Giorgio, begun 1565, Venice

The layout of the church of San Giorgio, built on the island of the same name opposite St Marks Square, was entirely original and is characterised by the succession of three distinct areas: the short nave and apsidal transept, the square presbytery with columns marking each corner and the monastic choir, separated from the presbytery by a screen of paired columns. The spatial articulation is also underscored by the different floor levels, subdivided by stairs, that lead the way from the entrance to the rear of the church in an ever-changing visual perspective. The façade of the edifice, featuring the device of the two intersecting classical pronaos was unfortunately not built until after Palladio's death — there is evidence of some incongruities in the pedestals elevating the supports, due to its tardy completion.

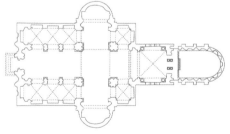

The two Venetian churches built by Andrea Palladio in his maturity are a definitive marker of the Renaissance genesis of religious buildings.

San Giorgio, designed in 1565 for the Benedictine Congregation of Santa Giustiana and the Redentore, commissioned by the Venetian Senate in gratitude for the deliverance from the Great Plague of 1575 –1576, are examples of Palladio's observance of the key Counter-Reformation dictates. Palladio, however, also established other new models for church buildings during his lifetime.

His experimentation with the intersection of orders, previously performed on the façades of secular buildings, took on a programmatic value on the monumental and magnificent Venetian churches, where the internal spaces are visually projected onto the exterior of the building by means of the classic temple-front elements featuring a double intersected order. Palladio's œuvre owed much to his studies of Bramante, Sangallo the Younger and Peruzzi, as well as to his logical interpretation of Vitruvius's obscure text on the double frontage of the Basilica in Fano, a building that greatly fascinated many Renaissance architects who were searching for examples of religious buildings in the treaty to emulate. Palladio's commitment to the ancient models is also illustrated by the interiors of both churches, where the grandeur of the Roman *thermae,* combined with a post-Tridentine liturgical approach, results in a harmonious hierarchical marriage of the spaces.

Andrea Palladio, view and plan of the Redentore, begun 1577, Venice

This great structure, built on the Giudecca, was commissioned by the Senate of the Republic of Venice and was given to the Capuchins after the plague in 1576. Its layout is consistent with its function as a votive church. The Doge and Senators instigated an annual procession of Venetian dignitaries, who traditionally filed into the nave in a lengthy and magnificent procession up to the large *tribuna* where they gathered beneath the dome to pray. The façade of the Redentore is undoubtedly far superior to that of San Giorgio as it adheres more closely to the classical model of the ancient temple. The larger pronaos sits above a majestic flight of stairs, which frames the main portal along with a superimposed attic inspired by the Pantheon.

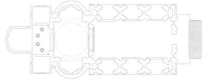

Andrea Palladio, interior of the Redentore, begun 1577, Venice

The spatial sequence in the scheme for San Giorgio becomes more complex in the Redentore, not least because of its important role in hosting the lavish annual procession. Three chapels open out of each side of the coffered nave, which leads to the *tribuna* with its two broad apses. It was here that the dignitaries could take part in the mass from a preferential position. The altar, positioned below the cupola, is screened from the choir by four freestanding columns arranged in a semi-circle, which also obscure the access to the twin square sacristies whose volumes protrude from the rear choir and serve to accentuate the cross-form of the basilica.

THE RENAISSANCE
IN EUROPE

The 16th century witnessed the definitive affirmation of the great European monarchies. France, Spain and Austria grappled for power to the detriment of the local feudal lords and city-states. The expansionist policy of absolutist rulers dragged the Italian states through a lengthy period of domination by France and Spain, who were thus exposed to the latest developments of the Italian Renaissance. Moving through France to Spain, classical codes slowly penetrated all the way up to the northern European regions, where political and religious problems and the decimation of territories put a halt to any significant departure from the Gothic aesthetic. Gothic codes survived all the way through the cinquecento, co-existing with the latest trends in a kind of stylistic co-existence.

Palais de Fontainebleau, begun 1527, France

The first earnest exploration of Renaissance principles outside of Italy was carried out in France, where François I's interest in classical art had already sparked a steady flow of labourers and architects from Italy to the court of Valois. The spread of architectural writings — particularly the tremendous Europe-wide success of Sebastiano Serlio's treaty, first published in 1537, with its fine illustrative woodcuts of ancient and modern architecture — marked a turning point. Northern European architects were thus able to gain an understanding of the classical models and the correct use of orders, laying the foundation for their own autonomous decorative style, perfectly tailored to the ostentatious French court. In Spain, however, a far more modest inter-pretation of Renaissance aesthetics was established in an expression of Philip II's Counter-Reformist spirit, which found its greatest expression in the im-posing Escorial complex.

opposite page
Antiquarium, Munich Residenz, 1569–1571, Munich

Munich, capital of Bavaria from 1505, became Germany's main artistic and cultural hub under Duke Albrecht von Wittelsbach, an adherent of the Counter-Reformation with ties to the pontifical circles in Rome. The Antiquarium (Hall of Antiquities) at the Wittelsbach residence, built by Friedrich Sustris to house the Duke's vast collection of sculptures and antiquities, still forms the core of Munich's museums. The enormous barrel-vaulted hall with its monumen-tal lunettes is sumptuously and elab-orately decorated with grotesques, reminiscent of the Roman cinque-cento and is one of the most success-ful architectural achievements of the German Renaissance.

Detail of the courtyard elevation at Château d'Ancy-le-Franc, begun 1542, France

Antoine III de Clermont commis-sioned Serlio to build a castle 'in the Italian manner' after 1541. The square plan and perfectly symmetrical chateau is built around a magnificent central courtyard with a complicated and sophisticated system of girders, reminiscent of Bramante's designs for the Belvedere. Arches on the ground floor, some open and some blind, the broad first-floor window openings, which rest directly on the cornice itself are flanked by pairs of fluted pilasters and are arranged on a plinth.

THE RENAISSANCE IN FRANCE

The classical vocabulary was introduced to France by Charles VII, who brought a group of artists (including Guido Mazzoni and Fra' Giocondo) back with him to France from the 1495 war in Italy and was consolidated with Louis XII's seizure of Lombardy in 1499.

The most influential personality in France's artistic renaissance was François I de Valois, who was also responsible for Leonardo da Vinci's move to Amboise in 1516, where he lived until his death three years later in 1519. François I regarded highly the importance of courtly life and surrounded himself with Italian artists who were requested to transform royal country estates throughout France, where the King and his entourage habitually lived in gilded isolation from Paris. Leonardo da Vinci, Andrea del Sarto, Rosso Fiorentino, Primaticcio and Serlio all had a seminal influence on French art, which, until then had been deeply entrenched in late Gothic models. These artists became the first to disseminate the classical culture beyond Italy.

Until the mid-cinquecento, however, the linguistic renaissance only applied to castles built for the king and for the aristocracy, while religious architecture took a while to transform, remaining tied to Gothic architecture throughout the 16th century.

**Château de Chenonceau,
1515–1524, France**

This huge castle in the Loire Valley
was built by Thomas Bohier, treasurer
to the French monarchy, with links to
François I, on what remained of an
ancient mill on the banks of the River
Cher. The walls of the chateau were
built by French labourers with the latest details executed by the Italian
artists in charge of the finishings and
ancillary decorations. This division of
labour was to become an accepted
practice in the construction of French
châteaux.

**Palais de Fontainebleau,
begun 1527, France**

The renovation of François I's
favourite residence was entrusted to
the architect, Gilles Le Breton, who
built an elongated gallery linking the
rooms to the private chapel. The decoration of the royal gallery was
entrusted to Francesco Primaticcio
and Rosso Fiorentino.
Philibert De l'Orme had the new wings
of the castle built as well as the spectacular Cour du Cheval Blanc, with its
magnificent double horseshoe staircase.

following pages
**Château de Chambord,
begun 1519, France**

The residence nestled in the middle of
Chambord Forest, is undeniably the
most successful of François I's castles. The enormous complex is built to
a strictly symmetrical plan, achieved
through the juxtaposition of six
square modules, which determine the
surface area of the building. Abutting
one of the long elevations is the *don-
jon*, a fortified bastion, which is itself
split into four sections by a spectacular central double helix staircase.

129

THE FRENCH NATIONAL STYLE

The early spread of the classical vocabulary in France was triggered by the Italian artists who imported Renaissance codes, although these failed to be taken up immediately by the French architects. Building methods rooted in the methodology of the Middle Ages and the challenge of understanding the *all'antica* lexicon meant that it was not until the mid 16th century that an autonomous national style was developed. The single event that evidently sparked the establishment of a French classical language was the meeting between Philibert De l'Orme (1510–1570), the most gifted French architect of the cinquecento and Sebastiano Serlio, who had resided in France since 1540. Serlio's contribution was fundamental, not so much for his rather meagre architectural output, as for the powerful influence of his treaty, which became a key point of reference for the shaping of a French classical language. The decision by François I to reject Serlio's design for the Palais du Louvre in 1546 in favour of the design by Pierre Lescot (1515–1578) officially heralded in the age of a new class of French architects, well versed in the classical Italian lexicon. The ascent to the throne of Henri II in 1548 saw Philibert De l'Orme's promotion to superintendent of royal buildings. De l'Orme was to remain in the service of the French monarchy for twenty years, making a significant contribution to the establishment of French classicism. De l'Orme's personal acquaintance with ancient ruins as well as the architecture of Bramante and Raphael is tangible in the Château d'Anet of which, sadly, little remains.

Philibert De l'Orme, entrance to the Château d'Anet, 1547, France

The Château d'Anet, built over a preexisting complex in Normandy for Henri II's mistress, Diane de Poitiers, is deeply reminiscent of the Roman classicism that De l'Orme had studied during his Italian sojourn. The lower section of the monumental entrance portal reinterprets the triumphal arch device, with a grand opening, framed by paired columns which support a classical entablature. The vocabulary employed for the second floor is less formal; this two lower levels are surmounted by an attic and a group of sculptures depicting a hunting scene, in homage to Diana.

**Pierre Lescot, Louvre, Cour Carrée,
begun 1546, Paris**

The wing of the Louvre overlooking the
Cour Carrée, aptly known as the Lescot
Wing, is characterised by a classical style
derived directly from Italian prototypes.
The double order of pilasters frames a
series of arches on the ground floor and
gabled windows on the upper floor.
Lescot's interpretation to the classical
language allowed for a series of diver-
sions, which were, however, to come to
typify French architecture: the subdivi-
sion of the long façade by projecting volumes emphasised by paired supports
and a high attic which rises from the central body of the building, partly masking
the traditional French sloping roof.

THE RENAISSANCE IN SPAIN

Unlike France, the political situation in Spain was only to stabilise towards the end of the quattrocento. The marriage between Isabella and Ferdinando in 1469 led to the first unification of the national territory, which was brought to completion when the Catholic kings took the final Arab stronghold, Granada, in 1492. The protracted war against the Moors and the ensuing financial crisis prevented Spain from implementing the kind of building developments appropriate to a great power. It was not until Charles V achieved political stability that the classical language began to flourish. Charles V had inherited territory in Spain, Austria and France as a consequence of his family's international matrimonial arrangements. He was educated in Flanders before moving to Spain, where he strove to modernise the medieval aesthetic of the places he passed through with his court. The palace in Granada, built by Pedro Machuca from 1527, was sensational and contemporary transplant of Renaissance Roman architecture into Spain and paved the way for the spread of a starkly monumental type of classicism, which was officially adopted in the mid 16th century when Prince Philip took over the building site. The evolution of Spanish architecture under Philip II's absolutist and rigidly religious stance reached its pinnacle with the Escorial Palace complex.

bottom, left
Pedro Machuca, courtyard of the Palacio de Carlos V, 1527, Granada, Spain

The wonderful circular courtyard leading to the palace rooms is configured by a double colonnade, Doric on the bottom level and Ionic on the upper level, which supports continuous entablatures rather than the typical 'order plus arch' scheme. The architectural vocabulary of the building is *all'antica* and absolutely in keeping with contemporary Roman models by Raphael and his piers. The circular scheme, which also features in some of Antonio da Sangallo the Younger's projects, would appear, in this case, to have been inspired directly by Villa Madama, built just a few years earlier by Raphael and suggests that Machuca may well have travelled to Italy.

Juan de Herrera, church of San Lorenzo in the Palacio del Escorial, from 1574, Madrid

The Escorial church was built as the imperial mausoleum for the Hapsburg sovereigns by Juan de Herrera, who became chief of works at the palace in 1572. Herrera's design was chosen by Philip II after he had rejected submissions from leading Italian architects, including Tibaldi, Alessi and Palladio, whose work was undoubtedly familiar to Herrera and had a substantial influence on the final design.

Juan de Herrera, view of the exterior of the Escorial, 1562–1584, Madrid

Philip II's decision to erect a huge religious complex in the Sierra de Guadarrama dates back to 1559. Apart from fulfilling one of his father's last wishes, which was to build a monastery where he could be buried with his wife, the establishment of the complex also served to commemorate Philip II's resounding victory against the French at the Battle of San Quentin on August 10, 1557, the Feast of St Lawrence. The works were entrusted to the royal architect, Juan Bautista de Toledo, who designed the general layout and were carried forward by Juan de Herrera from 1572, who completed the immense complex twelve years later, in 1584. The San Lorenzo el Real de Escorial convent is an extraordinary marriage of building typologies, determined by the diverse different functions of the building: monastery, fortress, royal palace, imperial mausoleum and religious retreat for the king making it one of the most extraordinary religious achievements of the Spanish Counter-Reformation. The gigantic rectangular volume, which measures over two hundred metres along its longest elevation, is completely covered with grey granite and has a massive tower projecting from each corner, which gives the impression of a fortified city rising above the plain.

NORTHERN EUROPE

Northern Europe — unlike France and Spain, both great Catholic monarchies tied to Italy by political, financial and cultural interests — took time to adjust to the Renaissance language, remaining largely faithful to the medieval throughout the 16th century. The territorial fragmentation of the Netherlands, part of which came under Spanish rule, coupled with Germany's devastation by the brutal Wars of Religion, meant that any cultural exchanges that might have attracted Italian artists to the north to disseminate the Renaissance classical language, were thwarted. Despite his study of classical culture, northern Europe's chief literary and humanist figure, the Dutchman, Erasmus of Rotterdam, was living in a society governed by medieval mores and traditions, where social life and artistic production were the preserve of the guilds. It was in towns like Augusta, at the intersection of the trade routes between Italy and Flanders and one of the wealthiest 15th century cities in Germany, that common ground between the new Italian style and the deep-rooted local traditions could be found. The classical repertoire became a means of social promotion for the wealthy bourgeoisie, who commissioned works where influences from the Renaissance vied with ingrained national conservatism. The publication of the first architectural treaty in Germany, the *Quinque Columnarum Exacta Descriptio atque Delineatio* by Hans Blum in 1550, was the means by which northern European culture was finally able to access and spread the *all'antica* ethos and open the flood gates of classicism.

opposite page
Ottheinrichsbau, 1556–1559, Heidelberg, Germany

The building constructed within the fortified medieval complex of Heidelberg during the cinquecento is named after the man who commissioned it, Ottheinrich Prince of Pfalz, who promoted the introduction of humanist studies and culture in Germany. The façade of the building, which was devastated by French troops in the late 17th century, is articulated by classical-style orders and decorated with sculptures in the round, reminiscent of the pronounced medieval *all'antica* decorative motifs.

Cappella Fugger, Church of Sant'Anna, 1509, Augusta, Germany

The extremely powerful Jacob Fugger, a dynamic personality in Germany during the early cinquecento period, was financier to Charles V and Leo X. Fugger financed the building of the family chapel in the church of Sant'Anna in 1509, which is generally considered to be the first religious Renaissance piece of architecture in Germany. The chapel is an eloquent example of the influence of the typical northern European Gothic style by incipient classical influences: the nave is characterised by the order framing the side arches in shapes that derive from Venetian churches, whilst the vault with its latticed rubs remains utterly Gothic, resulting in an unexpected contrast of styles.

THE NEW FINANCIAL HUB: ANTWERP

Emperor Maximilian transferred commercial privileges from Bruges to Antwerp in 1488, triggering the swift and dynamic economic development in Antwerp. The town became even more important strategically once the Americas had been discovered and the lucrative trade in precious metals on the new Atlantic routes had turned the port of Antwerp into the most modern of all European commercial hubs. The steady population rise, which stood at 87,000 in 1516, meant that the old 1410 city walls became too constricting, thus triggering a building frenzy that was to transform the face of the city over a twenty year period. The Italian architect, Donato Pellizuoli from Bergamo, was given the task to build a new fortified city wall in 1540, when the urban development grew beyond the city limits. Maria of Hungary, the sister of Charles V, governor of the Netherlands, became deeply involved with the plans to build new districts in the expansion area according to rational, modern dictates and asked the planner, Gilbert van Schoonebeke, to design a workable geometric urban plan. Van Schoonebeke also built the market square for the trading of grains.

Philip II's crushing of the attempts at rebellion in northern Europe, however, disrupted Antwerp's urban expansion programme and led to its inevitable decline. The Antwerp experience was still a seminal milestone for urban planners during the second half of the cinquecento and paved the way for further experimentation in urban planning for the upper classes.

Pierre van der Borcht, Antwerp Stock Exchange, 1567

Antwerp's massive economic and demographic development caused a great many public buildings to be constructed for utilitarian purposes at key points in the city. The Stock Exchange was built by Dominicus da Wagemaker in 1531 to a square plan, with rooms grouped around a large porticoed courtyard.

Cornelis Floris, Town Hall, 1561–1566, Antwerp, Belgium

The town hall in Atwerp, built by Cornelis Floris (1514–1575), is a classical solution to the medieval scheme consisting of a traditional central frontispiece. The façade, articulated by two superimposed orders of pilasters rising from a rusticated, arched base, reworks Italian plan formats and was probably inspired by an illustration by Sebastiano Serlio. The measured configuration of the side wings is offset by the decorative plasticism of the three central spans, which rise above the roof in a typically Nordic triangulated scheme.

THE ELIZABETHAN ERA IN ENGLAND

As with the rest of northern Europe, England was late to discover the classical language of the Renaissance, the vertical Gothic style remaining the architecture of choice. England's physical, political and cultural distance from Italy, exacerbated by the Reformist crisis, made England one of the slowest nations to embrace classical models, which only really became established during the 17th century. However, the stability bestowed on the country by the Tudor dynasty and the huge wealth accumulated by the aristocracy following the seizure of Church lands, together with the country's commercial traffic, gave rise to a national style during the reign of Elizabeth I that manifested itself in the building of opulent buildings for the most illustrious families, their defensive aspects softened by English aesthetic tastes. The stark perpendicular Gothic style of the enormous late 16th century English residences eventually began to incorporate classical motifs, not directly traceable to Italy, but filtered through the French and Flemish experiences and the architectural treaties circulating at that time.

opposite page
Courtyard of Burghley House, 1585, England

The monumental Tudor-style palace commissioned by Lord Burghley, one of Elizabeth I's ministers, near Stamford, contains an unusual courtyard, built in 1585, which is reminiscent of French architecture and the Château d'Anet in particular. The courtyard decoration was shipped directly from Antwerp and imbues the building with an entirely Flemish feel.

Longleat Castle, 1568, England

Sir John Tyne's residence at Longleat in Wiltshire, was designed by Robert Smythson, one of the greatest exponents of Elizabethan architecture and is characterised by its sober, measured decoration. The long façade is articulated by projecting elements that enliven the elevation and provide light to the internal apartments through large, typically English, bay windows. The spatial organisation of the surfaces is configured by the superposition of orders — Doric, Ionic and Corinthian, with pilasters framing the apertures and supporting perfect *all'antica* entablatures.

INDEX OF PLACES

PHOTOGRAPHIC CREDITS